Live Life in Full *Bloom*

Devotions to transform your ordinary path from the mundane and the mayhem into extraordinary living with Christ.

Bloom Daily Devotional Series
Book 2

Mary Rodman

Copyright © 2019 by Mary Rodman

All rights reserved. No part of this book may be reproduced or used in any manner without written permission of the copyright owner except for the use of quotations in a book review.

For more information, go to www.MaryRodman.com/

First Paperback edition July 2019

Cover design by: SelfPubBookCovers.com/RLSather

Photos included by:
Christine Lynn Photography, Plain City, Ohio

Published by:
Legacy Lane Publishing
Weatherford, TX
www.LegacyLanePublishing.com

ISBN: 978-1-7331234-0-2

To Jim,

Sometimes our lives consist of the mundane and the mayhem, but God has blessed this crazy life we live. Thank you for your endless support, endless love, and countless hours of patience as I write and speak about Christ. "Nothing's Gonna Stop Us Now" as we continue to *Live Life in Full Bloom* with Jesus.

> *A person standing alone can be attacked and defeated, but two can stand back-to-back and conquer. Three are even better, for a triple-braided cord is not easily broken.*
> *Ecclesiastes 4:12*

What readers are saying...

What a beautiful devotional book! I love the wonderful stories Mary weaves throughout the book. She is a gifted writer sharing hope and the love of our God, who makes our lives far from mundane. Even in sharing about her bathroom remodel, she shares golden nuggets like, "I pray every drop of water from my new rain shower head will remind me Christ washes away my sins." Awesome!
- *Doris Swift, Author of "Goodbye, Regret: Forgiving Yourself of Past Mistakes"*

A good devotion or devotional book contains elements of nostalgia, scripture, actionable faith, relatable life circumstances and something to discern in my own life. Mary does a masterful job in her craft of checking these boxes. As an agriculture business, we are proud to now *Live Life in Full Bloom* as Mary already shared with us how to *Bloom Where You're Planted*.
- *Integrity Ag Group, Heath Conklin and Michael Rushing*

Live Life in Full Bloom leaves you with…a sense of happiness, hope and sense of peace of God's love and understanding. Mary's work is easy to read, and her devotional will touch your life in a similar way."
- *David C. Thorbahn*

Table of Contents

How to use this devotional 2

Thank You 3

A thank you gift for you… 5

About the Author 6

Foreword 10

Introduction 11

Give It Your All 14

White Iris 16

Toilet 19

Deep Roots 21

God's Love 23

Lord's Prayer 25

Wonderful Creations 28

Bloom 30

Dance and Celebrate 33

Fog of Confusion 35

Snow Angels 38

Teachable Moments 40

Peppermint Patty 43

Who Are You? 45

Grandpa Said No 47

Flowermonia 49

Nothingness 51

Under His Wings	54
Seriously	56
Father-Daughter	58
Rosie	62
Hair Style	65
Bathroom Remodel	68
Life Is a Journey	71
Does He Notice?	72
Partnership	75
Ground Sparrow	78
Generations	80
Sad Memory	83
Get Out of Your Box	85
Be Strong and Immovable	87
Long-Distance Friends	90
Why Me Lord?	92
The Cleaver Family	95
Rotisserie	97
Sweet Aroma	100
Garbage Dump	102
Encouragement	105
Fire of Blessings	108
Catch Your Dirt	111
Play-Doh	113
Childhood Confession	115

Bluebirds and Mimosa Trees	117
Disgusting Tasks	120
Gnarly or Smiling	122
Rules and Grace	124
Old Friends	126
Overstuffed	128
Dare to Dream	130
The Fall and The Rise	132
Break the Silence	135
The Donkey	137
The Storm	140
Zip-Line	141
Happy Anniversary	143
Sandcastles	146
Follow Christ More	149
The Fire	152
Sorry Grandma	155
The Key	158
The Rock	161
Lost Cell Phone	163
Shattered Window	165
Reflection	167
Leah's Dedication	169
Pelican	171
Social Media	173

Donnie	176
The Breeze	178
Flea Market	179
Bottle of Wine	181
Deception	184
What's Your Handicap?	186
Give Everything	189
Raindrop	191
Email Blunder	194
Glitter Stones	197
Wild Flowers	199
In the Year 2525	201
Out on A Limb	203
Thunder	205
Killdeer	207
Abundance	209
Dirty Truck	211
Tough Love	214
Zucchini Crisp	216
Dullbozer	219
Snuggles	221
Leap of Faith	223
Artesia Geyser	225
The Move	227
Combine Repair	229

Underfoot 231
Dale 233
Difficult Decisions 236
Memorabilia 238
Compassion for the One 240
Conclusion—New Beginnings 243
Resources 246
More books and resources 250

How to use this devotional

Your devotional can be used in multiple ways.
- You can read it like a book, as you enjoy one God story after another.
- Read one devotion each morning and allow God to speak to your heart throughout your day.
- You can randomly select a topic of interest each day, allow God to lead you to the title of choice for your morning devotions.
- Read the book with a friend or a group. Conversations and discussions with others will always provide more insight on the topic. You will be amazed how each devotion speaks differently to others.
- Journal your thoughts each day. There are sample pages from my ***Live Life in Full Bloom Journal*** at the end of the book. You will find a Daily Gratitude section which challenges you to focus on a new blessing each day. You can purchase the accompanying journal at www.MaryRodman.com/shop.

Thank You

Until you begin to put words to a page and pages into a book you never realize exactly how many people are involved in a project.

My family and friends often set the stage for my devotions and I thank each of you for allowing your lives to be an open book for God's glory. The life we live together and the stories I share become God moments to touch the lives of others.

As the journey continues, acquaintances not only become friends, they become sisters in Christ. Thank you, *Diane K. Bell of Legacy Lane Publishing* for your marketing and publishing expertise. I am forever grateful for the knowledge you shared and our wonderful conversations as we worked together on this project.

God set the wheels in motion many years ago when he brought *Rev. Dick Smyers* to our small country church. Thank you, Pastor Dick, for leading me to the Lord as a young teenager and for still calling me "the kid" after all these years. The impact you made upon my life has now trickled down into the lives of others.

Your daughter Christine Dillion came to my rescue with her beautiful photography. Thank you, *Christine Lynn Photography* for the perfect pictures for the devotions, "Social Media" and "Bluebirds and Mimosa Trees."

My readers, how do I even begin to thank you for the blessings you have bestowed upon me? Prior to publishing my first devotional, *Bloom Where You're Planted*, I had only shared a few of my devotions with others. As a result of their encouragement I sought publication and my life began to change. My intentions were to bless the lives of others with my thoughts about God's presence in our everyday lives, but I received more blessings than I ever gave. I was soon overwhelmed by the reviews I received with kind words such as: "I love the way Mary uses everyday life experiences to connect with God. She has a gift for writing and her short devotionals are 'just right' for a daily read." ~*Nancy Bowman*

> "We all have moments of frustration with whatever our current life-path is…Although each devotion focuses on a different area, the theme is the same: You aren't where you are by accident. Seek God fully and see what He has in store for you there." ~*Kindle Customer*

> "Mary does an excellent job of using real life experiences to connect with God. I would highly recommend this book to anyone who needs a word of encouragement or a way to look at everyday experiences in the light of God's grace." ~*Angie H*

Words like these and others, have blessed my life beyond measure. I soon realized that God had bigger plans than a devotional book. My ministry began to grow and I made the decision to *Live Life in Full Bloom* wherever God leads. God has blessed me with a "retirement career" I love—writing and speaking about Jesus!

No thank you would be complete without also saying, "Thank you *Jesus Christ* for allowing me to *Bloom* as we walk this crazy adventure together. From the mundane to the mayhem You are forever a present of my life."

A thank you gift for you...

- Download these free products at www.MaryRodman.com/BookBonuses.
    - *Inspire U* Stay in touch by using our messenger's treasury of transformational inspiration, insight, and guidance. **Download and join** the free *Inspire U app* for additional personal resources on your mobile device today!

    - *Lessons from Peter* A collection of devotions about Peter from *Bloom Where You're Planted.*
    - *Blessings* Devotions from *Bloom Where You're Planted* to bless your life.
    - *Mary Magdalene—A Woman of Resilience* An abbreviated version of the Bible study which walks through the life of Mary Magdalene as she was transformed from a woman possessed by seven demons into a resilient servant of Christ.

Serving Him Always,
Mary

About the Author

Mary resides in Radnor, Ohio with her husband, Jim. Together they enjoy farm life, hard work, vacations, family and friends. She is a farm girl at heart who discovered her niche as a Christian author and speaker. Mary loves to share about the Lord through both her written and spoken words. Mary's life is an open book as she shares her joys, her struggles and embarrassing moments.

As a member of the Central Ohio Emmaus Community, Mary finds joy in helping others cultivate and grow their relationship with the Lord.

She is the author of the devotional book, *Bloom Where You're Planted*, which "is a wonderful gift for those strong in faith and those just 'blossoming' (Anonymous)." Her devotional books are a journey through her life. You will laugh and cry as you relate to Mary's day to day life with Jesus. Her unique style of writing intertwines the gospel with her easy to understand stories. Her devotional formats vary and leave you searching for more. They include—Points to Ponder, Suggested Scripture Reading, a few poems, and even a recipe created in her own kitchen. *Bloom Daily Devotional Series Book 1, Bloom Where You're Planted* can be purchased at www.MaryRodman.com/shop.

Purchase your matching journals! These are only available at www.MaryRodman.com/shop. *Bloom Where You're Planted Journal* and *Live Life in Full Bloom Journal* each contain a "Daily Gratitude" section with a quote from the daily devotion. It is a great way to track your thoughts as you look for God's presence in your daily life.

Bloom Daily Devotional Series Book 3 is *Bloom in God's Promises*. It will be available in the future, but tidbits of encouragement from the book will be shared at:

www.MaryRodman.com/BookBonuses and on social media, just follow the links at www.MaryRodman.com.

Book Mary as a Speaker-Facilitator for a Weekend Retreat
Who Are You? Discover the woman God created you to be.
Proverbs 31:29 "There are many virtuous and capable women in the world, but you surpass them all!"
www.MaryRodman.com/speaker

"When we were looking for someone to talk at our fall women's retreat, someone mentioned Mary Rodman. I did not know Mary at the time, but have since come to see her as a friend and Sister in Christ. We meet with Mary and talked about our retreat and what we were looking for and gave her the theme. Mary ran with the theme and gave us not only talks but small group questions and devotions for each session. The attendees found the talks relevant to our lives and the small group questions meaningful and thought provoking. Would definitely use Mary for a retreat again and would highly recommend her to speak at your retreat." *~Shirl Hensel Co-Chair, Women at the Well, Trinity Lutheran Church, Marysville, OH*

- Mary's retreat will transform your walk with Christ as she shares her funny stories, biblical examples, and powerful messages. The topics include:
    - **Defining Moments** Are there really any bad defining moments in your life? Mary challenges you to look at your bad defining moments in a positive light when used as a witnessing tool for Christ. Biblical story: Woman caught in adultery.

- o ***God Loves You*** God loves the woman He created you to be—exactly like you are, with all your flaws, gifts, talents and idiosyncrasies. Biblical story: Samaritan Woman.
- o ***Who Are You?*** Mary challenges you to envision yourself as the person Christ created you to be. Biblical story: Mary Magdalene.
- o ***Dare to Dream*** Regardless of the defining moments in your life God loves you unconditionally. You are God's chosen, precious, beloved, royalty so dare to dream of ways to serve Christ. When you align your dreams with God's will for your life amazing ministry will transpire. Biblical story: Caleb.
- The weekend retreat is available in multiple formats.
    - o Mary as a speaker only. She will present the four talks and provide breakout questions for your small group leaders in advance.
    - o Mary as both the speaker and the facilitator for your event. At the end of each talk, she will facilitate questions and discussions with a larger group of ladies.
    - o Optional music by Angie Howard. Angie's musical talent as a worship leader and soloist is uplifting and inspirational.

Book Mary as a Speaker – She provides transformational messages on a variety of topics.
- ***Something Out of Nothing*** While in a season of grief Mary discovered she could make something out of nothing which changed her outlook on life. She will help you find blessings on those most difficult days of grief.
- ***Dare to Dream*** *"What you dare to dream of, dare to do." Sarah Jane Shoaf.* Learn how to follow your dreams and

be motivated to accomplish them by aligning your dreams with God's will for your life.

- ***Bloom Where You're Planted*** God calls us to—Bloom through adversity. Bloom with joy. Bloom in the silence. Bloom in Spirit. Mary shares biblical truths through her stories of humor and heartache.
- ***The Woman God Sees*** *"The Lord delights in you." (Isaiah 62:4).* Mary's personal stories and scripture will lead you through these four biblical truths: You are Chosen. You are Precious. You are Loved. You are God's Royalty.
- ***A Christian Farm Wife's Perspective*** As a woman who wears many hats, from farmwife to speaker and author, Mary shares her struggles as a newlywed on the farm and how they learned to build their marriage around Christ even on the most stressful days.
- ***Faith, Farming and Career*** As a farmwife Mary shares farm statistics to increase awareness of the family farm. She incorporates how faith, farming, and her career as an author and speaker all intertwine and work together for God's glory.
- ***Custom Topic*** All of Mary's speaking topics are a result of special requests. She is open to speaking opportunities on your topic of choice. Please allow a minimum of six-weeks preparation unless previous arrangements have been made. For more information, please contact Mary at: www.MaryRodman.com/speaking.
- Book Mary as a speaker for your next event at www.MaryRodman.com/speaking.
- To learn more about Mary as a speaker, to follow her on Social Media, or purchase her books, follow the links at www.MaryRodman.com.

Foreword

So Who is Mary Rodman and why should you make these devotionals part of your daily walk with God?

I believe the best answer to both these questions is best stated by Mary herself:

"I am Mary Rodman, who was saved by God's grace. I am a simple, beautiful, humble, gifted, disciple of God, whom He chose to write my crazy stories, intertwine them with scripture and share with the world." (Taken directly from the devotional within these pages, "Who are You?")

Mary's passion for life and living according to God's Word is self-evident in each and every story she weaves…Stories from her own humble daily life with family and friends.

Her divine gift? "Seeing" teaching moments in everyday mundane events. She then pivots them into humorous, divinely inspired devotions…each designed to capture your heart and bring you joy as you're gently reminded of God's grace in your life.

I've been privileged to share the final part of this journey with Mary. It's been an honor to help her publish this book and guide her to include special gifts for you. Be sure to visit her website and pick them up here.

www.MaryRodman.com/BookBonuses

And think of Mary when you're looking for an inspirational speaker, or a facilitator for your next weekend retreat…you'll be glad you did!

Diane K. Bell/ Publisher-in-Chief
LegacyLanePublishing.com

Introduction

We recently remodeled our master bathroom. One of the first steps in the project was the removal of a six-foot-wide mirror from the wall. It now leans against our bedroom wall, but it has been rotated. Instead of being six-foot-wide, it is now six-foot-tall which gives me a totally different perspective than before. We do not intend to leave it there permanently yet I have grown accustomed to the benefits of a tall mirror.

This mirror gives me the opportunity to reflect upon my physical appearance. I can see an entire outfit from head to toe and decide if it looks appropriate for the occasion. Sometimes I stand in front of the mirror with a selection of jewelry to make a decision. Unfortunately, I also see the aging process taking place quicker than I would like. But according to *Job 12:12, "Wisdom belongs to the aged, and understanding to the old."* So, if aging gives me wisdom, I will take it all in stride.

What my mirror can't show me is my inner beauty, my wisdom, or my soul. No man-made item can show these items only a sovereign God has this ability. Our souls are a deep part of us which can only be strengthened through a relationship with Christ. We often neglect our own soul even though the condition of our soul will determine our outlook on life.

The Biblical wisdom referred to in Job is not wisdom you and I just stumble upon. Our relationship with Christ directly impacts our wisdom, which in turn affects the condition of our soul. Much like your relationships with your spouse, friends, or co-workers, your connection with Christ needs nurtured. You have to continually work on your relationship to make it stronger.

In his study, *Soul Keeping*[i], John Ortberg says, *"We live in a world that teaches us to be more concerned with the condition of our cars, or our careers, or our portfolios than the condition of our souls. Maybe because a dent in a soul is more easily concealed than a dented car. Maybe because a dented soul is harder to fix. After a while, the dents pile up, and they stop bothering us. We hardly notice. One dent more isn't going to make much difference."*

Just like the directionnel change of the mirror gave me a new perspective of myself, Jesus is the only One who can give us a new perspective on the condition of our soul. Ortberg goes on to say, *"I am responsible to take care of my soul not just for my own sake. The condition of my soul will affect the people around me, just as when my body is sick. It can infect others who get too close."*

On a scale of 1-10: 1 your soul is in utter turmoil and 10 your soul is in excellent condition and connected to God, what number would you select?

In order for us to care for our souls we need to have a healthy relationship with Christ. Solomon tells us *"The Lord grants wisdom! From his mouth come knowledge and understanding." (Proverbs 2:6).* Even though the Lord grants us wisdom, we have to seek and desire it. A relationship with God is no different than a relationship with a loved one. It can wither, be stagnant, or grow and bloom.

My first book, *Bloom Where You're Planted*, was a set of devotions written to help you see God in your everyday life. *Live Life in Full Bloom* is the same principle. It's not about the mutation of a purple iris to a white one, or a baby bird which startled me, or my brother-in-law's new toilet (all devotions in this book). The stories are simply a means to see God in every aspect of our lives. In return, our relationship with the Lord will grow. This growth will give us a healthier soul. A healthy soul will help you focus on the promises of God and bloom in your ministry.

In *Live Life in Full Bloom* every devotion will be different. Some will contain the scripture, others will only share the reference. The length will vary and the platform will change. The variety leaves the challenge up to you. You have the choice to make. Do you desire to know God more? Will you take the relationship further and dig deeper each day to fill a void in your soul? Or do you allow the moment to pass and simply whisk it away with the other clutter in your life? As you read each devotion, allow the message to resonate in your heart. Ask Jesus to open your heart to its significance or a passage of scripture. I pray you will rate the condition of your soul a little higher on our scale of 1-10 by the time you read the conclusion.

Mary's unique style of seeing God in her everyday life is evident in *Bloom Daily Devotional Series Book 1, Bloom Where You're Planted*. It contains 99 devotions which will empower you to look at your path of the mundane and the mayhem differently. Purchase a copy today at www.MaryRodman.com/shop.

Give It Your All

At a recent event known as the Walk to Emmaus I was blessed to be on the leadership team and help lead discussions with some wonderful ladies. On our last day, we asked one another about our favorite Bible story. For me it was so hard to choose. You have the story of Esther. The Samaritan Woman. The woman who touched Jesus' robe. Peter walked on water. How do you choose just one? I admit I don't remember which one I selected, but I remember Iola's favorite. It was the widow woman's offering.

This short story in the Bible wasn't even on my top ten list, so when Iola mentioned this story it piqued my interest. I have always felt that Jim and I are good financial stewards, so these few verses never made much of an impact. I always read them with pride in my heart. Give financially, yep done, checked off my list of good deeds. What an attitude, because the story is about much more than financial stewardship!

> *While Jesus was in the Temple, he watched the rich people dropping their gifts in the collection box. Then a poor widow came by and dropped in two small coins. "I tell you the truth," Jesus said, "this poor widow has given more than all the rest of them. For they have given a tiny part of their surplus, but she, poor as she is, has given everything she has." Luke 21:1-4*

I read these verses several times over the next couple of days, and studied the footnotes in my Bible. God calls for us to give our all. Not just financially, but in every area of our lives. I am now convicted every time I read, *"For they have given a tiny part of their surplus, but she, poor as she is, has given everything she has."* Jesus calls us to give all of our time to serve others. All of our strength for the trials in life. All of our compassion for the hurting. All of our gifts and talents. In every area of our lives, we should take intentional steps to give all we have to Christ.

In these verses, Jesus isn't concerned about a money issue. He is concerned about a heart issue. The widow wasn't blessed because she gave financially. She was blessed because she gave from her heart. She reminds me of David, a man after God's own heart. (*1 Samuel 13:14*). She was a woman after God's own heart. She wasn't a woman who simply gave monetarily. She was a woman who invested in the kingdom of God with all of her heart, all of her mind, and all of her soul. *(Matthew 22:37).*

> Dear Lord,
> I ask your forgiveness for my foolish pride and for the time I spend on worldly items, which do not point others to Christ. Change my heart Lord, so I desire to serve You with my whole heart, my whole mind, and my whole soul. Help me to use my gifts and my talents within your church, and the ministries which bless You. Lord give me strength to go above and beyond what I feel is possible each day, because with You everything is possible. Please help me grow stronger in my faith and become a Christian who desires to see others as You see them. Make me more like the Widow Woman and turn me into a woman who is after God's own heart. You have asked for my best Lord, and for today, I give You my all.
> In Jesus' name, Amen.

White Iris

The flowerbed beside our driveway is full of iris. One variety has a small, dark purple bloom. Today when I looked at all the beautiful purple flowers, I did a double take. Right in the middle of the purple iris was a single white iris bloom! I have never planted white iris at my home, so I considered it a gift from God. The white bloom stood out amongst all of deep purple flowers. It was so radiant and I quickly snapped a photo to show a couple of my friends.

As I scurried about my evening routine, I reflected on the white flower and looked at the picture numerous times. The white flower is a symbol of so many biblical truths. Color mutation—God is the creator of everything. Yesterday, today and tomorrow. He created the white iris from the genetics of a purple one. White—the color of purity. Jesus was the only pure person to walk this earth, and with His purity comes an opportunity for us to have eternal life. Single flower—let your light shine. Be who Jesus has called you to be in this world. Even when you are the only white flower in the crowd, show it boldly. My white iris beautifully illustrates this scripture.

In the beginning the Word was with God,
and the Word was God.
He existed in the beginning with God.
God created everything through him,
and nothing was created except through him.
The Word gave life to everything that was created,
and his life brought light to everyone.
The light shines in the darkness,
and the darkness can never extinguish it.

(John 1:1-5)

    The gospel of John helps us understand that the Word, or Jesus, existed from the beginning. God created everything through Him. From the mountains to the seas, the flowers to the birds, He created it all. He is still in the creation business today, just like He created a white iris from purple ones. Just as the white iris is a new creation, we are a new creation in Christ. *(2 Corinthians 5:17)*.

You often see portraits of Jesus dressed in white. White is a symbol of purity. He was sinless, without flaw, and perfect in every way. Through His perfection, He provided redemption for our sins. His death and resurrection, *"brought light to everyone." (John 1:4b)*. The white iris reminds me of the old hymn, "What can wash away my sins, nothing but the blood of Jesus.[ii]" This perfect Lamb of God washed away our sins so we may be pure and white, just like the white iris.

Once you accept Jesus as your Savior, the Light is part of your life and the darkness slowly fades. Difficulties will come your way. The loss of loved ones. Financial struggles. Divorce. Rebellious children. Crying babies. However, no circumstance you face is in total darkness. He is the true Light in a dark world. Christ is your White Iris in a flowerbed of worldly problems.

There is the twist in the story though. The next day I had two white irises. The third day three and this morning I have white iris blooms in several places. This is an example of the glory of Christ! When you shine your light in a dark world, you show the love of Christ. Soon others are led to His amazing grace and Christians multiply like the white irises in my flowerbed!

As you scurry about your daily routine, focus on the White Iris called Jesus. He is still and will always be in the creation business. He is the Light of the world. His Light will shine bright in the darkest moments of your life. So, continue to celebrate your salvation and shine your light for Jesus!

Toilet

During our recent visit to Florida, my brother-in-law Bumpy was proud to show off his new toilet. Prior to our arrival, their friends had come to visit and stayed at their home for about a week. On the second day of their visit, the gentleman announced, "Bumpy you need to fix this toilet. It sits too low."

As is typical of Bumpy off to the hardware store they went to purchase a new tall toilet. Not only did he purchase a new toilet, but he also purchased a special toilet seat for his guests. Why a special toilet seat you ask? All because his friend's wife didn't like the seat which came with the toilet. By evening, the toilet had been replaced.

My reaction to this situation was one of shock. I wanted to say, "Are you kidding me! They are guests in your home, and they have the audacity to complain about the height of the toilet and request a special toilet seat? How ungrateful!"

Not Bumpy. He never felt they were rude or ungrateful in any manner. He shared the toilet upgrade story with a chuckle and a smile on his face.

How many of us look at life with a Bumpy attitude? We often allow our "right to be offended" control our emotions. We get upset when someone crosses the line, or is inconsiderate, ungrateful, or just simply rude. Bumpy could have easily become angry at their request, but he chose to look at the positive side of the situation. A new toilet and special toilet seat. Plain and simple. No reason to be offended.

Paul challenges us to live a life which allows us to overlook the flaws of others and to live life with a Bumpy attitude.

Since God chose you to be the holy people he loves, you must clothe yourselves with tenderhearted mercy, kindness, humility, gentleness, and patience. **Make allowance for each other's faults, and forgive anyone who offends you.** *Remember, the Lord forgave you, so you must forgive others. Above all, clothe yourselves with love, which binds us all together in perfect harmony. And whatever you do or say, do it as a representative of the Lord Jesus, giving thanks through him to God the Father. (Colossians 3:12-14,17 - Emphasis added)*

One of the hardest lessons in life is to allow for one another's faults and offer forgiveness. The toilet lesson taught Jim and I to have a Bumpy attitude in life. When one of us gets upset or offended by someone's actions the other one says, "remember the toilet." Which simply means, it is trivial and unimportant, so let it go and see the good in the situation.

These verses remind us to model Christ with our words and our actions. It isn't always the easiest attitude to take, but it is what we are called to do. Next time you are offended by someone, say to yourself, "remember the toilet" and have a Bumpy attitude in life.

Deep Roots

Just down the road from us is a bridge which crosses the Scioto River. As you cross the river and look you will see a tree which has become its own island. I suppose over time the river shifted and caused it to stand alone. Every time the flood waters come; I wonder if this big tree is strong enough to withstand the rush of the water. So far so good because the tree still stands after the spring floods.

Right now, the water level is low and I can see part of the tree's root system. I honestly don't remember this before. All of the floods this year must have washed away more dirt from around the roots. I have observed root systems before but I am fascinated by this one. I suppose it is the size, or maybe the fact I have been intrigued by this tree for over a year. The roots are massive, strong, and woven together in a ball. All of these roots look like a huge, tangled, gnarly maze, yet they support the tree through flood after flood.

In order for us to *Live Life in Full Bloom,* we need deep roots intertwined with Christ. Those roots are strengthened when we follow Jesus instructions found in *1 Corinthians 13:13. "Three things will last forever—faith, hope, and love—and the greatest of these is love."* These three promises will give us the roots to withstand the storms in life and to endure those moments when agony floods our souls.

Faith isn't just a one-way stream it flows both directions. God is faithful to His believers as we read in *Lamentations 3:23.* *"Great is his faithfulness; his mercies begin afresh each morning."* But Jesus also calls us to trust in Him. *"The Good News shows how God makes people right with himself—that it begins* and ends with faith. As the Scripture says, 'But those who are right with God will live by faith.'" *(Romans 1:17 NCV).*

Max Lucado eloquently describes faith. *"Faith is the belief that God is real and that God is Good...It is a choice to believe that the one who made it all hasn't left it all and that he still sends light into the shadows and responds to gestures of faith[iii]."*

Paul says we need more than faith, we also need hope. *"We put our hope in the Lord. He is our help and our shield." (Psalm 33:20).* God commands us to hold tight to Him on those difficult days of life. Don't ever lose hope, because our hope is in Christ. He is in control and knows how much we can withstand! Faith ties us to this hope, because if we have faith in the scriptures, we are able to read about the hope God provides. *"The Lord is good to those who hope in him, to those who seek him." (Lamentations 3:25 NCV).*

Faith, hope and love. Love ties it all together. It is the heart of what it takes to be God's disciple. *"So now I am giving you a new commandment: Love each other. Just as I have loved you, you should love each other. Your love for one another will prove to the world that you are my disciples." (John 13:34-35).* Love encircles faith and hope. Just as the flood water circles the tree, love circles our lives. Our faith and hope give us the ability to love when we don't feel it is possible. We suddenly see others through Jesus' loving eyes.

God is the Living Water for our souls. He is the Way, the Truth and the Life, *(John14:6)* upon which we need to build a massive, strong, deep, tangled, maze of roots. Hold tight to your faith and allow Jesus to be the root system in your life. When the storms of life come and the flood waters rage, remember your hope is in Christ Jesus! Allow His love to encircle you so you can love others in all the circumstances of life.

God's Love

Did you ever notice that the longer you know someone the more alike you become? On most days, I can finish my husband's sentences or even know what funny comment he is about to make. I find the longer we are married the more alike we become and the more I love him.

No matter how well we know and love our spouses, our children, or our best friend, it is nothing compared to how well God knows us and loves us! The Bible tells us, *"The very hairs on your head are all numbered. So don't be afraid; you are more valuable to God than a whole flock of sparrows." (Luke 12:7).* Just imagine how well He knows you to have numbered the hairs on your head!

Jeremiah 1:5a (MSG) goes on to say, *"Before I shaped you in the womb, I knew all about you. Before you saw the light of day, I had holy plans for you."* I have made many mistakes in my life yet God approves of me with all of my flaws!

Just as my husband woos me, God woos us. He longs to have a relationship with us. No sin we have committed is too great to keep us from His love.

When children misbehave, they instinctively run and hide from their parents. No matter whether you hide temporarily or a long time, you hide because you feel unworthy of love. In either situation, a child knows there is unconditional love in the arms of their parent and they eventually return.

This is much like our relationship with Christ. We are God's children who ask for forgiveness from their Father. Sometimes it's easy to ask for mercy and other times we question why Christ would forgive us for all we have done. Nothing you and I do will ever keep us from the love of God. He will always forgive all our sins, if we simply return to His arms of grace. *"There is forgiveness of sins for all who repent." (Luke 24:47b).*

This is my prayer for you today, *"May the Lord direct your heart into God's love and Christ's perseverance." (2 Thessalonians 3:5 NIV).* If you don't know Christ or if you walked away from him, please take time to pray and ask him for the forgiveness of your sins. Abba Father longs to hold you close and have a relationship with you.

Lord's Prayer

Our Father
The Ancient Father of Abraham, Isaac and Jacob is also the Father of you.

Which art in heaven,
God is seated in heaven where the streets are made of gold and the gates are made of pearl.
You are Majestic and Your glory shine so bright.

Hallowed be thy name.
Abba, Father, Precious One, Healer, Shepherd, Comforter, Adonai.
You are Holy, Omnipotent, Righteous and Just.

Thy kingdom come,
One day soon your kingdom will come again.
There will be a new heaven and a new earth where You will reign forever.
There will be no more evil. No more pain. No more suffering.

Thy will be done
Lord, have Your will with me here on this earth. Here. Now. Today.
I give you my life. Take me and use me for your glory.
Teach me to be a witness of your greatness.

On earth as it is in heaven.
As I reach out to an unsaved world, may I be more like Jesus.
Please Lord, use me on this earth to love others.
Help me represent a heavenly love.

Give us this day our daily bread.
Thank you for my provisions for today, tomorrow and always.
You give me nourishment, strength, hope, and fill me with Your power.
When I am filled with your Holy Spirit, I am able to do unfathomable feats in Your name.

And forgive us our debts,
Lord, forgive my many sins. Both those I am aware of and those I am not.
Help me to continually seek and remember your grace.

As we forgive our debtors.
Help me to forgive others as you have forgiven me.
Give me the strength to be your instrument of love and grace, to people who need Your forgiveness.

And lead us not into temptation,
Keep me from the unrighteous path. Do not allow me to stumble.
Please put a hedge of protection around me and my family from the evil one.
Protect your ministries and your churches from Satan.

But deliver us from evil.

Lord when I do stumble, put a path before me so I may be delivered from Satan's destruction.
Give me strength to persevere and wisdom to choose the path of righteousness.

For thine is the kingdom
Your kingdom. Your heaven where You reign on high.

And the power
Your strength. Your almighty power which we cannot comprehend.

And the glory forever.
Glory. Radiance. Brilliant Light.
Your glory which will shine without end forever and ever.

Amen.
Thank you, Jesus, for you are the last word and so it shall be.

(Matthew 6:9–13 KJV)

Wonderful Creations

My son Ryan and I love to send one another the Snapple "Real Fact[iv]" which you find on the bottle caps of their products. Real Fact #860 says, "Dolphins sleep with one eye open." #1031 is "An octopus has three hearts." Some facts give us a chuckle, while others provoke deep thought and questions. For example, how do they know dolphins sleep with one eye open? I do not understand how you research and discover this fact. On the other hand, why did God give the octopus three hearts? Do they need three to supply enough blood to all of their arms? God made such a unique world. The stars and planets, seas and mountains, trees and plants, mammals, fish and birds, each one is different.

We are surrounded by unique creations each day, from the sea creatures to our friends and neighbors, we are all distinctive. The dolphin and the octopus have amazing qualities. God knew the dolphin needed to sleep with one eye open, and the octopus needed three hearts. In *Genesis 1:20-21* we read where God said, *"'Let the waters swarm with fish and other life...' So God created great sea creatures and every living thing that scurries and swarms in the water...And God saw that it was good."*

For us to create or build an object it requires research and a great deal of time as we build a plan. But God is so amazing He simply spoke this world into existence. And to top it off, they weren't just created, they were created perfect. Each animal has the right number of hearts and the perfect instincts to protect themselves. Our finite minds cannot comprehend the infinite capabilities of God. We simply can't fathom all He is capable of creating.

The greatest part of the creation story took place on the sixth day when God created humans in His image. *(Genesis 1:27).*

Once again, He created each of us unique, special and perfect. But don't miss the important message in the next verse which sets us apart from other creations.

> *Then God **blessed** them and said, "Be fruitful and multiply. Fill the earth and govern it. Reign over the fish in the sea, the birds in the sky, and all the animals that scurry along the ground." (Genesis 1:28 - Emphasis added)*

God said all He created was good, but He only blessed the humans. We were created in God's image with a soul so we would crave fellowship with Him. When He blessed us, He set us apart from all other creations. Worship God with a thankful heart today for you are His creation. Thank Him for the uniqueness of this world with all of its wonder and beauty. Most of all be grateful you were created in His image, unique, set apart, and blessed by God.

Suggested Scripture Reading
- Genesis 1

Bloom

So here's what I want you to do, God helping you: Take your everyday, ordinary life—your sleeping, eating, going-to-work, and walking-around life—and place it before God as an offering. Embracing what God does for you is the best thing you can do for him. Don't become so well-adjusted to your culture that you fit into it without even thinking. Instead, fix your attention on God. You'll be changed from the inside out. Readily recognize what he wants from you, and quickly respond to it. Unlike the culture around you, always dragging you down to its level of immaturity, God brings the best out of you, develops well-formed maturity in you. (Romans 12:1-2 MSG)

I visited a different church Sunday and the pastor closed with the scripture above. I am familiar with this passage of scripture but not from *The Message*. As I followed along, I highlighted the reference so I could focus on it later. As I reread the passage again it occurred to me, the reason this scripture spoke to my heart is because it is the theme of my books! Bloom! Stop what you are doing—the daily grind—and focus on God.

Often times we walk through life in a blur. Our daily lives become routine. You brush your teeth, grab your coffee, and drive to work. Routine is good, but look beyond your routine for the aspects of God. He is everywhere, every day. He is even with you in the dull daily routine. He doesn't want your life to feel monotonous. He wants you to feel alive.

The next time you brush your teeth, thank God for the toothpaste on your brush. Thank Him for the job (whether you like it or not) which provides the money to purchase your toothpaste. Are you stuck in traffic? Take a look around. Do the other drivers look happy, sad, frustrated? Rather than post the traffic jam on social media, say a prayer for them as you patiently wait. Is there a long line at the coffee shop? Have some fun, pay it forward and purchase for the car behind you.

Rather than constantly asking God, "What do you want me to do?" Get involved where you are—BLOOM today. God isn't waiting for you to go on a mission trip to Zimbabwe. He wants to use you at this current moment in your life and in your current circumstances. Include God in your day to day, routine, humdrum, life because, *"If you are faithful in little things, you will be faithful in large ones." (Luke 16:10a).*

By all means have hopes and dreams to serve God in big ways. I believe He desires for us to grow and plan for the future, but He also expects us to accept our current situations and see Him in the small pieces of life.

God wants you to be patient and focus on Him, so you will learn to bloom. Once you begin to see God the small parts of your life, you will find yourself able to *Live Life in Full Bloom*! When you live this way, when you understand God is with you all of the time: *"You'll be changed from the inside out."* You will begin to grow and serve in ways you can't even imagine. Amen!

Like the sunflower,
Live Life in Full Bloom,
and serve Christ, even in the wood pile!

Dance and Celebrate

While babysitting my granddaughter Reagan I turned on the television so she could watch *Mickey Mouse Clubhouse*. When the television came on it was tuned to *Little House on the Prairie*. Reagan was about one at the time and was immediately drawn to the television. She intently watched the girls play and dance in the school yard. Much to my surprise she began to play and dance with them. Together they had quite a celebration. It was fun to see her play with the girls as if they were in the room with her.

God calls us to dance and celebrate as well. *Psalms 149* and *150* says to celebrate with harps, tambourines and dance. The Old Testament is packed full of celebrations such as New Moon Celebrations and Passover Celebrations. When Solomon became king, they celebrated. *(1 Kings 1)*. In Old Testament days, they celebrated when God performed a miracle. But the New Testament calls us to participate in the greatest celebration of all, the salvation of a lost soul.

Luke 15 (MSG) has three parables to remind us to celebrate when a sinner returns to Christ. The Lost Sheep, The Lost Coin and The Prodigal Son.

> **The Lost Sheep** *When found, you can be sure you would put it across your shoulders, rejoicing, and when you got home call in your friends and neighbors, saying, "Celebrate with me! I've found my lost sheep!" Count on it—there's more joy in heaven over one sinner's rescued life than over ninety-nine good people in no need of rescue.*

The Lost Coin *And when she finds it you can be sure she'll call her friends and neighbors: "Celebrate with me! I found my lost coin!" Count on it—that's the kind of party God's angels throw every time one lost soul turns to God.*

The Prodigal Son *"Quick. Bring a clean set of clothes and dress him. Put the family ring on his finger and sandals on his feet. Then get a grain-fed heifer and roast it. We're going to feast! We're going to have a wonderful time! My son is here—given up for dead and now alive! Given up for lost and now found!" And they began to have a wonderful time.*

We celebrate when our team wins the Super Bowl. We have graduation celebrations. We have birthday parties. Many churches even celebrate the end of Vacation Bible School with a party or a carnival. But we do very little to recognize those who commit their lives to Christ. There is joy in heaven when the lost sheep returns, and the parable of the Lost Coin tells us the angels rejoice when the lost return. The Father has a party when the prodigal son returns home. Like the gospel of Luke explains, salvation should be a time to rejoice and to celebrate. So, let us celebrate!

The next time you hear the good news of one's salvation remember Reagan and the girls from *Little House on the Prairie*. Join them as you dance and celebrate the salvation of one of God's chosen lambs!

Suggested Scripture Reading
- *Luke 15*
- *Psalm149, 150*

Fog of Confusion

My husband, Jim, and I are faced with a difficult church decision. We feel as if our church has gone astray from the basics of Christ. We see emphasis put on the props, the stage, the fancy programs and the extravagant Vacation Bible School. But we don't see Christ and the power of prayer in the midst of all the glamour. In addition, the pastor has boxed me into a position where I cannot use my gifts and passions. With all this confusion, we have many questions for God. If our church isn't a prayer driven, God centered church—do we leave, or do we stay and help make a difference? Do I continue to work where my ideas and passions are squelched, or does God have a greater plan and vision for us elsewhere?

Throughout our search for answers, I have read many books and of course the Bible. I would like to say we have made a decision, but in all honesty, it changes daily. One day God says flee from a church which is not focused on the power of prayer. The next day, God says we should stay and make a difference. Maybe all of this confusion is God's way of saying, "Be patient my children."

When I walk in the mornings, this decision is often the topic of my conversation with God. One morning God gave me a clear picture of what our confusion looks like. The morning sun was beginning to shine over the wheat field while the fog still lingered in the air. What an example of how I feel in this fog of indecision. Yet in the midst of the fog, I can see the Son!

Every Sunday morning, we ask ourselves, "Where shall we attend church today?" God has made several choices clear to us. We desire a church where the gospel is preached and the ministry is bathed in prayer. At the end of the church service we don't want our focus to be on how talented the musicians were, or the beautiful set, or even how dynamic the pastor spoke. We want a worship experience which points us toward Christ. One where we are excited to go and share the gospel with a lost world.

In all of this confusion and fog in our minds, we know the Son is in our midst. He has a plan for our lives and we need to follow where He leads. For now, our answer is to take time to heal and patiently wait upon the Lord. Every church we visit touches our hearts and brings us one step closer to a new church home. Every prayer we speak, brings us one step closer to God and His desire for our lives.

"Jesus said to Simon, 'There is nothing to fear. From now on you'll be fishing for men and women.' They pulled their boats up on the beach, left them, nets and all, and followed him." (Luke 5:10-11 MSG).

With every prayer and every Sunday morning decision, we remember Simon left all he had and followed Jesus with no fear. On this Sunday morning, we have no direction except to follow where Christ leads us today, and not to fear what the future holds.

Snow Angels

Last week we had the first snow flurries of the season. My granddaughter Mya was so excited. She stood at the sliding glass door for a long time to watch the snow fall. Several times with great enthusiasm she said, "It's snowing Grandma!"

This week we had our first real snow with an accumulation of about two inches. We were at Dad's house when the snow began to come down. The traffic was slowing down, so immediately after lunch I packed up my granddaughters to head home. I buckled Reagan into her car seat, turned around and saw an excited four-year-old flat on her back in the snow.

"I'm making a snow angel," Mya exclaimed as her arms and legs went back and forth in the snow.

"Yes, I see but you don't have on snow boots. I hope you don't get cold before we get home."

I brushed off the snow, buckled her into the SUV and we headed for home. As I predicted the drive was slow, but we made it safely. Looking back, I wish I had taken Reagan out of the SUV and let her make a snow angel with Mya. Mya was ecstatic about the first snowfall of the season, but I was worried about the slow cautious drive home. A few minutes for Reagan to make a snow angel would not have made any difference in our travels. I allowed my worrisome, over protective, Grandma instincts take over and missed a fun moment with my granddaughters in the snow.

The Lord longs for us to let go of our worrisome, over protective instincts and make snow angels with Him. Don't miss opportunities to spend time with Jesus daily.

"You are more valuable to God than a whole flock of sparrows." (Matthew 10:31). So, allow God to care for your worries and problems.

Some of my most precious moments in life are when I am able to teach my grandchildren about Jesus. If I had made snow angels with them, I could have taught them to be thankful for the snow and the fun it provides.

Jesus too loved children and said, *"Let the children come to me. Don't stop them! For the Kingdom of Heaven belongs to those who are like these children." (Matthew 19:14).* When you have the opportunity, set your worries aside, and make snow angels with the children you love. Have a great time, but remember to teach them about Jesus too!

Teachable Moments

Sometimes four-year-olds can surprise you. They think differently than we do as adults. Some days we just need to go with the flow and hope for the best. Today was one of those days. I told my granddaughter Mya to look at all the pretty orange and yellow leaves on the trees. She was quick to respond, "I love the red ones."

To which I replied, "I just love fall and all of the beautiful colors."

In excitement Mya said, "I love Christmas!"

I was sure the reason she loved Christmas was because of the presents and so I asked, "Why do you love Christmas?"

"Because of the snow," she replied.

Normal conversation up to this point, but this is where the conversation takes a turn because I didn't let it drop. My mind thinks—teachable moment, do not miss this opportunity. This is where a four-year-old mind can outsmart an adult every time. You could not have prepared me for her reply when I said, "I thought maybe the reason you love Christmas is because it is Jesus' birthday."

After a short silence she asked, "Hey Grandma, if it is Jesus' birthday, how does He blow out His candles?"

At this point I need advice fast and I begin to pray, "Lord, I'm doing my best work here, can you help me with this one?"

"Mya, you know how it is windy outside today? Well, Jesus makes the wind so I'm sure He can blow out His birthday candles too," I replied.

"Grandma, if Jesus can't blow out His candles it's okay. I will help him!"

If there had been no wind as an example of God's amazing powers, I don't know how I would have answered her question about His birthday candles. I love the innocence of Mya's question and wonder what can we learn about the wind which helps us with our adult situations in life.

God sent the wind to dry up the floodwaters for Noah. *(Genesis 8:1)*. The wind blew from the east and brought locusts during the plagues on Egypt. *(Exodus 10:13)*. It blew once again and parted the Red Sea to save the Israelites. *(Exodus 14:21)*. Then the Israelites experienced the power of God through the wind as it brought quail for them to eat in the wilderness. *(Numbers 11:31)*. Psalms, Proverbs and Ecclesiastes all mention the wind numerous times, but the story which spoke to me the most concerning the wind was found in *Matthew*.

> *Then Jesus got into the boat and started across the lake with his disciples. Suddenly, a fierce storm struck the lake, with waves breaking into the boat. But Jesus was sleeping. The disciples went and woke him up, shouting, "Lord, save us! We're going to drown!" Jesus responded, "Why are you afraid? You have so little faith!" Then he got up and rebuked the wind and waves, and suddenly there was a great calm. The disciples were amazed. "Who is this man?" they asked. "Even the winds and waves obey him!" (Matthew 8:23-27)*

Over the past several weeks, the wind has blown and the storms have brewed in my life. I had a four-year-old mentality when it came to the storms in my life, instead of trusting Jesus. When I read this passage, I heard Jesus say deep in my soul, *"Why are you afraid? You have so little faith!"* If Jesus can calm the winds and the storms, He can handle the problems in my life. The answers are always right there, in the Word, to bring us peace.

Oh, to see life in the eyes of a child. God has taught me so much through my grandchildren. All too often we forget to look for those teachable moments when our lives are busy.

So, I must ask myself, "Who's teachable moment was it? Mine or Mya's?"

Peppermint Patty

My nephew Heath, and his wife, Trisha, are expecting their second daughter. They live in Kentucky, and as a result their family in Ohio patiently waits for updates. One day they asked for name suggestions on Facebook. They had settled on Patricia for a middle name, after Heath's mother. Heath joked that he liked Peppermint Patty, but Trisha would not allow him to use that name! The name suggestions flowed in and so did the jokes. Brat Patty, Chicken Patty, and my husband picked TwoAllBeef Patties and Cow Patty. The poor baby girl had horrible nicknames and she wasn't born yet. In all seriousness, a lot of wonderful names were suggested. I personally thought Mary Patricia had a nice ring to it, but Maebree Patricia was their ultimate choice.

Last weekend the doctors decided to move the process along and admitted Trisha to the hospital. They induced labor but it was unsuccessful! After hours of hormones and Pitocin, Peppermint Patty refused to leave her safe haven. Trisha was dismissed from the hospital as they patiently (somewhat) await the arrival of Peppermint Patty. Obviously, it was an emotional experience for them, but they continue to find their strength in Jesus. Heath continues to find humor in the situation and says it is like the movie *Groundhog Day*. He wakes every morning praying for labor, but there is no change.

Their patience was tested last weekend and I can't imagine the emotional ups and downs they experienced. The labor would start and then stop. God frequently tests our patience in many of life's situations. We question. We beg. We pray. We begin to see changes, and then the changes stop. Sometimes we even try to solve the situation ourselves, which is never a good idea.

As Christians, what are we called to do when the frustrations of life build? Pray. *"The humble will see their God at work and be glad. Let all who seek God's help be encouraged. For the Lord hears the cries of the needy." (Psalm 69:32-33a).* Whether you are impatiently waiting for labor pains, or you feel the pain of a difficult situation in your life, remember God is with you. When you seek the Lord, you will always find the strength you need for each day.

I reminded Heath and Trisha they were in our prayers and shared this scripture with them. *"We also pray that you will be strengthened with all his glorious power so you will have all the endurance and patience you need. May you be filled with joy." (Colossians 1:11).* Whatever you are patiently or impatiently waiting for in your life, I pray these words will bring you, patience, comfort and joy as well.

Who Are You?

While leading the communion meditation Pastor Kathy asked numerous times, "Who are you?" Every time she asked the question, she looked directly at me. I started to get a little paranoid. I leaned toward my friend and whispered, "Why does she always look at me?"

She replied, "I don't know but I was wondering the same thing."

In the same manner that Pastor Kathy presented the question that evening I am asking you, "Who are you?"

When Pastor Kathy first asked the question, I thought to myself, "I'm Joe Conklin's daughter." A phrase I have proudly said all my life. Other thoughts included: Jim Rodman's wife, Matt and Ryan's mom, Bill's sister, author, grandma, friend. All the while I was missing the point. What Pastor Kathy wanted each of us to understand is who does Christ say we are.

I will ask you again, "Who are you?" Was your reply similar to my initial thoughts or did you describe yourself as the person God sees? A child of the King. God's chosen child. Daughter. Precious. Beautiful. Blessed. Believer. Beloved. Humble servant. Disciple.

I spoke with Pastor Kathy later and discovered she did not look directly at me or even my direction intentionally. That is the power of the Holy Spirit at work in your life when you are squirming in your seat with conviction! God wanted me to understand the message. My thoughts on this question did not end that night either. I pondered "Who are you?" as I drifted off to sleep. I continued to think about it when I woke and as the day progressed. I began to contemplate scriptures and search for more Bible verses which truly described who I am as God sees me.

Once you had no identity as a people; now you are God's people. Once you received no mercy; Now you have received God's mercy. (1 Peter 2:10)

Jesus said to the people who believed in him, "You are truly my disciples if you remain faithful to my teachings." (John 8:31)

Yet God has made everything beautiful for its own time. (Ecclesiastes 3:11a)

Humble yourselves before the Lord, and he will lift you up in honor. (James 4:10)

Thank God for this gift too wonderful for words! (2 Corinthians 9:15)

Have compassion on me according to your great and unfailing love. (Nehemiah 13:22b)

After significant time and thought I came up with a godly definition of who I am. Not how I see myself but how God sees me with my God given gifts and talents.

I am Mary Rodman who was saved by God's grace. I am a simple, beautiful, humble, gifted, disciple of God who He chose to write my crazy stories, intertwined with scripture to share with the world.

One last time I ask, "Who are you?" Spend some time and truly pray about this question. Search the scriptures for verses which describe how God feels about you and His desire for your life. Because, *"Who knows if perhaps you were made queen for just such a time?" (Esther 4:14b)*.

Grandpa Said No

I babysit my granddaughters two days a week. On Tuesday, we have lunch with my dad who they call Grandpa Joe. Grandpa Joe is the keeper of the gummy worms. The cookie jar is always full and usually they can find cheese puffs or caramel corn. Reagan who is not quite two even knows the routine. We drop her sister, Mya off at preschool. When we pull in his driveway she says, "Grandpa Joe's house." We visit. She eats junk food, then we pick Mya up from school, and return for lunch.

One particular Tuesday I was washing the lunch dishes when Dad returned to the kitchen. Reagan was playing with the key in the antique secretary desk at the time. Grandpa Joe saw what she was doing and said, "No." He wasn't gruff. He wasn't abrupt or mean to her. It was just a simple, "No." She was somewhat disobedient, because I had to tell her no again just a few moments later.

After dishes were put away, we loaded into the car and headed for home. As we pulled out of his drive Reagan began to pout and said, "Grandpa Joe said no." He had rocked her world! The keeper of the gummy worms corrected her for the first time EVER. How could he possibly say no? I repeated the story to her mom and dad later in the day, and she immediately pouted again. It was obvious Grandpa Joe hurt her feelings.

As adults, we are much like Reagan when God tells us no. We question His reasons. We doubt His plan and direction for our lives. We live in a society where "No" is not the norm. If you want a perk in life, no need to wait just go purchase it. We are told we deserve the best, the latest, and the newest of everything. And no need to worry about the outcome or impact on others, we live in a "me" society.

We need to remember God hears every prayer, but He answers prayers according to His wisdom. Even David laments about his unanswered prayer. *"Yet when they were ill, I grieved for them. I denied myself by fasting for them, but my prayers returned unanswered." (Psalm 35:13).* We shouldn't doubt God, but allow the situation to build a greater faith. What we want, is not always what God wants for us.

> *You want what you don't have... You are jealous of what others have, but you can't get it, so you fight and wage war to take it away from them. Yet you don't have what you want because you don't ask God for it. And even when you ask, you don't get it because your motives are all wrong—you want only what will give you pleasure. So humble yourselves before God. Resist the devil, and he will flee from you. Come close to God, and God will come close to you. (James 4:2-3, 7-8a)*

Like Reagan, we want to play with the key to our lives. We want the desires of our heart whether good or bad, but God wants what is best for us. The "no" is to help build our faith. Sometimes it is to protect us from what we do not know or understand. We need to use those moments as faith building lessons. Stepping stones to a time when Jesus will truly hand us the keys to heaven and say, *"Well done, my good and faithful servant...Let's celebrate together!" (Matthew 25:21).*

Flowermonia

My granddaughter Mya is a girly girl. She always has bows in her hair and polish on her nails which she is quick to flash for everyone to see. On this particular day, Mya had pink toenails with polka dots, white leggings, a flowered dress, and a bow in her hair.

She was lounged back in Grandpa's big recliner and asked me to play doctor with her. I grabbed a flashlight and checked her throat and ears. I felt her head for a temperature. Then I went to her feet and said, "Oh no, this could be serious you have pink toes with dots!"

She of course giggled and the fun continued. I worked my way up from her toes and said, "Pink toes, white legs and flowers growing out of your belly. This can be only one illness, flowermonia, and it is serious!" We continued to play as she giggled some more.

It was perfect timing, because I suddenly heard an ambulance in the distance. I told her an ambulance would come get her soon. She didn't notice the siren at first but as it became louder, she began to worry. "Grandma, we are just playing. It isn't coming for me, is it?"

Not to be mean, but so she would learn how to joke I said, "I don't know. We will just have to see."

Mya listened intently. The closer the ambulance came the bigger her eyes opened as she truly began to worry. I ended the joke and assured her it was not going to take her to the hospital.

Sometimes fear in our lives is not harmful. In Mya's case I inflicted a little fear so she would understand a practical joke. However, fear can be an emotion which controls us and does not allow us to be the person God created. Sometimes fear can even keep you from a life filled with joy. There are numerous scriptures which remind us we should not be afraid, but this verse is one of my favorites.

> *Fear not, for I am with you;*
> *Be not dismayed, for I am your God.*
> *I will strengthen you,*
> *Yes, I will help you,*
> *I will uphold you with My righteous right hand.*
> *(Isaiah 41:10 NKJV)*

This verse is very direct. It boldly says if we believe in God we have no reason to be afraid. In the past, I struggled with fear in my life. Fear of what others thought about me or how they would judge my actions. There are definitely times I did not live my life to the fullest due to fear. I was afraid to act a little crazy and enjoy some laughter for fear that someone might be critical of my actions.

When fear creeps back into my life, I remember *Isaiah 41:10* and God's promise to be with me. I refocus and find strength to enjoy the moment.

> *This is why I remind you to fan into flames the spiritual gift God gave you when I laid my hands on you. For God has not given us a spirit of fear and timidity, but of power, love, and self-discipline. So never be ashamed to tell others about our Lord. And don't be ashamed of me, either, even though I'm in prison for him. With the strength God gives you, be ready to suffer with me for the sake of the Good News. (2 Timothy 1:6-8)*

Do you suffer from flowermania or the fear of an ambulance? Are you afraid to follow Christ? Make *Isaiah 41:10* your key verse today as you focus on Christ rather than the fear of the unknown.

Nothingness

For the children's sermon on Easter Sunday the pastor gave each child an empty plastic bag. The children were excited and thought Easter candy would soon fill their bags. Then the pastor asked, "What is in your bag?"

"It's empty."

"You forgot to put something in here."

"Nothing."

"I didn't get anything."

One young boy said, "It is filled with a whole lot of nothingness."

The pastor and congregation chuckled at his creativity of nothingness. The empty bags were a representation of the empty tomb on Easter morning. A bag which usually contains groceries, candy, or toys was empty. The tomb which should have contained the body of Jesus Christ was empty. God's huge gift of nothingness for which we should all be grateful.

I can't help but think about your spiritual closest. Is it filled with a whole lot of nothingness or have you put on the full armor of God to fight the enemy?

As Christians, we are in a battle. Not with one another, not with our children, our spouse, or a pesky neighbor, but with evil powers. We are not equipped to handle these battles without the power of the Holy Spirit. In order for us to be strong we need to remain close to the Lord and walk with Him daily. The sermon you heard on Sunday is not the armor you need until next week! You need to fill your spiritual closet daily.

A final word: Be strong in the Lord and in his mighty power. Put on all of God's armor so that you will be able to stand firm against all strategies of the devil. For we are not fighting against flesh-and-blood enemies, but against evil rulers and authorities of the unseen world, against mighty powers in this dark world, and against evil spirits in the heavenly places. Therefore, put on every piece of God's armor so you will be able to resist the enemy in the time of evil. Then after the battle you will still be standing firm. Stand your ground, putting on the belt of truth and the body armor of God's righteousness. For shoes, put on the peace that comes from the Good News so that you will be fully prepared. In addition to all of these, hold up the shield of faith to stop the fiery arrows of the devil. Put on salvation as your helmet, and take the sword of the Spirit, which is the word of God. Pray in the Spirit at all times and on every occasion. Stay alert and be persistent in your prayers for all believers everywhere. (Ephesians 6:10-18)

Each morning, remember Jesus said, *"I am the way, the truth, and the life." (John 14:6).* Therefore, strap on the belt of truth. Follow God's commandments and put on your body armor. *(Psalm 119:172).* Remember you are a child of Christ and Satan cannot steal you back no matter what happens. *(John 10:28-29).* Your faith is your shield for battle. Faith is a gift from God so remember to stand strong against the enemy. *(1 John 5:4).* The battle has been fought and we are victors with Christ. Remember your gift of salvation as you go into battle. *(1 Corinthians 1:18).* Your sword, your defense, or your weapon against your enemy is to fight with the Word of God. Simply put, if you want to fight Satan fight him with scripture. Stand on the Book of Truth and pray in all circumstances. This will give you the best defense against Satan you can find.

Don't let a day pass and have your spiritual closet filled with a whole lot of nothingness. The tomb was filled with nothingness, with that knowledge you can withstand the battle against the evil one. Start each day with a full arsenal of God's gifts. Truth. Righteousness. Peace. Faith. Salvation. The Word.

Under His Wings

As I pulled weeds from the flowerbed, I was startled by a morning dove when it flew away. I let out a little scream bent down to continue and another one left. When I squatted down again, I saw a baby bird hidden among the flowers. It had apparently taken its first flight from the pine trees and didn't get far. I left him alone and moved further down the flowerbed. I am sure the morning dove parents were close and would soon return to protect their baby. I was amazed how they were all huddled together and camouflaged by the flowers.

When David was on the run for his life, he sought protection under the wings of God. He later wrote about his experience. *"Have mercy on me, O God, have mercy! I look to you for protection. I will hide beneath the shadow of your wings until the danger passes by." (Psalm 57:1)*. Even though David was on the run from Saul he had a band of people who followed him.

> *So David left Gath and escaped to the cave of Adullam. Soon his brothers and all his other relatives joined him there. Then others began coming—men who were in trouble or in debt or who were just discontented—until David was the captain of about 400 men. (1 Samuel 22:1-2)*

David became the captain of these men, many of which were scoundrels. He had to make a choice—become their godly leader or allow these men to influence him in an ungodly manner. David chose to be a godly leader. Saul continued to pursue David and every time he came close David turned to God for wisdom and direction. David hid under God's wings and grew in leadership, integrity, strength, wisdom and honor.

David and his men were hidden in a cave when Saul entered unprotected by his men. The band of scoundrels told David it was a sign from God and taunted him to kill Saul but David refused. Instead David cut off a piece of Saul's robe and later realized it was wrong to have done so. David forbids his men to harm Saul and spared Saul's life. *(1 Samuel 24)*. This truly shows David was a man after God's own heart. *(1 Samuel 13:14)*. He didn't allow his selfish ambition to hurt Saul. He relied on God's protection and waited for God's divine intervention in his life. When you seek refuge under God's wings it always pays off.

After the first incident with the birds I later returned to pull weeds in the flowerbed. Guess what? Yep—you guessed it! I was startled by a bird once again. Only this time it was just the baby bird as it flew directly back to the nest. All of his mini flights from the tree to the flowers had given him the strength and wisdom to protect himself.

The baby bird took refuge under the wings of Momma and Papa bird. In the same manner, David took refuge under the wings of God. If you feel you are lost in a wilderness or hidden in a cave, take refuge under God's wings. There you will find peace, strength, and wisdom for the journey ahead.

Suggested Scripture Reading

- *1 Samuel 22, 23, 24*
- *Psalm 57*
- *Psalm 17:8*

Seriously

Today I had to make one of those dreaded phone calls to cancel a subscription. You know the type. You go through five or six phone menus and hope you select the correct options along the way. With every menu, I thought, "How many menus does it take to reach a real person?" Then when I finally did reach a person, I couldn't understand her because of her heavy foreign accent. Seriously?

When I told the kind lady I wanted to cancel my subscription, she went into a sales pitch for a less expensive package. I promptly said, "No thanks. I'm not interested in your service even if it is twenty dollars a year."

She started selling once again. I explained, "We don't like the service and we need to cut expenses." Still she continued with her sales pitch. Seriously?

It was at this point I began to lose all of my Christianity. I was frustrated and it all started with the impersonal phone menus. I sternly told her I didn't like the service. I was not interested in a lesser package and to cancel my subscription—all in a not so nice tone. Then she informed me I owed a $5.10 late fee because the subscription renewed five days ago. I informed her that I received my statement only yesterday and lost the remainder of my Christianity. Seriously!

Since my notice was not mailed prior to the renewal date, she ultimately canceled my service and wrote off the late fee. I apologized—in a not so nice tone. Now I feel guilty for my not so nice attitude. Seriously.

The irony of the entire situation is my current Bible study is on the book of Ruth and I definitely did not live up to today's lesson on how to show kindness to others.

Ruth was a foreigner from the land of Moab. According to the Jewish customs, she should have been treated lower than Boaz's servants, yet he showed her kindness. Not only did he invite her to eat with the harvesters, he instructed the harvesters to leave some barley on the ground for Ruth to glean. As a result, Ruth worked behind them all day to fill her basket. *(Ruth 2:14-18)*.

Boaz, *"a wealthy and influential man in Bethlehem," (Ruth 2:1)* showed Ruth, the Moabite, great kindness. Mary, the author of this devotion, showed the foreign customer service representative disdain and impatience today. Seriously.

I am reminded of Paul's words in *Romans 7:18-20* where he says we want to do good, but because of our sin we aren't always successful. On frustrating situations like today, I wonder, where is the good which lives in me? Why did I grow impatient so quickly? Unfortunately, I have no way to undo my attitude with the lady on the phone or show her some kindness. Hopefully down the road, I can show kindness to others with the money I saved on an unnecessary subscription.

Ruth was a foreigner who provided for herself and Naomi by gleaning the fields. Boaz noticed her hard work and the love she had for her mother-in-law, so he rewarded her with kindness. Likewise, God will turn my bad attitude phone conversation into good, as He sees my heart's desire is to do what is good with my life. Seriously!

Suggested Scripture Reading
- *Ruth 2:14-19*
- *Romans 7:18-20*
- *Romans 5:14-16*

Father-Daughter

On the farm, we use FM radios to talk to one another from a distance. Today my son Matt is in the field around the corner and I have his daughters. Mya is old enough to use the radios so I told her to call Daddy and let him know we would soon bring lunch. When Matt replied, Reagan who just turned two ran to the radio saying, "Dada, Dada!" She waved her arms in excitement and smiled from ear to ear. She immediately jabbered in her own words telling Daddy lunch was on the way.

Matt works long hours and his full-time job requires quite a bit of travel yet Reagan knew the sound of his voice on the radio. It was obvious they have a special father-daughter bond. As I watched her excitement, I wondered how often do I get excited and enthusiastic to talk with my heavenly Daddy?

We are fortunate our heavenly Father works long hours. He is always home and excited to talk with us. He desires a Father-daughter (or Father-son) relationship with His children. He longs for us to come quietly and sit in His presence. You can come to cry or bring a smile and jabber enthusiastically. Others may come unsure of what to say and sit in silence. Are you upset with life? You can wave your arms and stomp your feet in frustration. Maybe you simply want to sing softly and whisper His name. He doesn't care how you come. He simply wants to spend time with you.

Reagan ran to talk to Daddy and I pray you run to your Heavenly Father. We should be excited and enthusiastic to build a Father-daughter relationship. I challenge you to find a special Bible verse about prayer which touches your heart. In my search, I came across "David's Prayer of Thanks." The acrostic "**STARS**" is demonstrated in this section of scripture. I hope David's prayer touches your heart as it did mine.

Sin
Thanksgiving
Adoration
Requests
Silence & **S**cripture

David's Prayer of Thanks

Then King David went in and sat before the Lord and prayed, "Who am I, O Lord God, and what is my family, that you have brought me this far? And now, O God, in addition to everything else, you speak of giving your servant a lasting dynasty! You speak as though I were someone very great, O Lord God!

"What more can I say to you about the way you have honored me? You know what your servant is really like. For the sake of your servant, O Lord, and according to your will, you have done all these great things and have made them known. O Lord, there is no one like you. We have never even heard of another God like you!

"What other nation on earth is like your people Israel? What other nation, O God, have you redeemed from slavery to be your own people? You made a great name for yourself when you redeemed your people from Egypt. You performed awesome miracles and drove out the nations that stood in their way. You chose Israel to be your very own people forever, and you, O Lord, became their God.

"And now, O Lord, I am your servant; do as you have promised concerning me and my family. May it be a promise that will last forever. And may your name be established and honored forever so that everyone will say, 'The Lord of Heaven's Armies, the God of Israel, is Israel's God!' And may the house of your servant David continue before you forever. O my God, I have been bold enough to pray to you because you have revealed to your servant that you will build a house for him—a dynasty of kings! For you are God, O Lord. And you have promised these good things to your servant. And now, it has pleased you to bless the house of your servant, so that it will continue forever before you. For when you grant a blessing, O Lord, it is an eternal blessing!" (1 Chronicles 17:16-27)

Sin—David starts his prayer as a humble servant. He knows he is unworthy of the greatness God has bestowed upon him. (*1 Chronicles 17:16-17*, **Paragraph One**)

Thanksgiving—He thanks God for the blessings he has received. (*1 Chronicles 17:18-20*, **Paragraph Two**)

Adoration—He speaks of God's wonders and miracles which He has already completed. (*1 Chronicles 17:21-22*, **Paragraph Three**)

Requests—At this point, David submits his will and his requests to God. Rather than ask God for his own desires he acknowledges God is fully in charge of every situation. (*1 Chronicles 17:23-27*, **Paragraph Four**)

Silence & Scripture—Though this prayer doesn't say David sat in silence or read the scriptures after his prayer, we do know David was a man after God's own heart. *(1 Samuel 13:14)*. Reread verse *16a* again, *"Then King David went in and sat before the Lord and prayed."* I believe, David, a man after God's own heart, spent time in silence and scripture before and after he prayed such beautiful words to the King of Kings.

Rosie

For the last month or so I have experienced some back problems, so it is a challenge to clean the house right now. Plus, our master bathroom has been under construction for several months, which creates extra dirt. Needless to say, the dirt has piled up, and I am overwhelmed. There is a new addition to our family and her name is Rosie. At first I was reluctant to bring her in, but I have come to love her. Rosie cleans about two hours a day and is an energetic little worker. Most days she does a pretty good job with the day to day dirt, while I clean other areas as much as my back allows. Wow, as I sit here at the kitchen table writing devotions, Rosie cleaned cracker crumbs which my granddaughter dropped yesterday. Way to go Rosie!

Rosie does have a few small problems. For example, lately she refuses to go under our bed! I think she is afraid of what is under there, and I can't blame her. Maybe the dust bunnies have actually come to life! I wish Rosie could read the Bible while she recharges. She would learn to overcome her fears with an increase of faith. If she understood God was with her, she would clean under the bed. *"So do not fear, for I am with you; do not be dismayed, for I am your God. I will strengthen you and help you; I will uphold you with my righteous right hand." (Isaiah 41:10 NIV).*

Another problem is that she tends to repeat herself. Those cracker crumbs she cleaned; she has been back three times! Enough already go clean under the bed. Her mission to clean the same area three times is better than those who spread the same piece of gossip three times around their church or neighborhood. Since Rosie cannot speak, she does follow the instructions of *Proverbs 10:18b, "Slandering others makes you a fool."*

She also loves to chew on shoe strings. Since I tend to drop shoes everywhere, this is a problem. She has taught me to do a daily roundup of my footwear. A little bit ago I heard this clomp, clomp, clomp as she moved around. "Oh my, she has my shoe again." I quickly came to her rescue and detached the shoe. Her burden was much lighter after its removal, and she is off and running again. *"Share each other's burdens, and in this way obey the law of Christ. If you think you are too important to help someone, you are only fooling yourself. You are not that important." (Galatians 6:2-3).*

Our house is a big open design with a lot of obstacles so Rosie gets lost occasionally. If I'm not home to supervise her progress, she will rest in the strangest places. Like under chairs or beds and stuck in corners. Sometimes she even gets frustrated with our area rug, stops, sulks, and beeps an error code. When she gets run down, she throws her hands in the air (if she had hands), stops for the day and takes a rest. *"Those who live in the shelter of the Most High will find rest in the shadow of the Almighty." (Psalm 91:1).*

Overall, Rosie is a good little robot house cleaner. If she decides to stay employed here for a year, she will cost less than fifty cents a day. At this stage of my life she is worth every penny. I hope she will stay a lot longer, as we continue to work on our relationship and her cleaning skills.

Yes, Rosie is a good financial deal, but God has the best deal available for all. For free, He will calm your fears and increase your faith. As for gossip and other sins, He will wipe the slate clean. Heavy burdens? God will lighten your load. He provides you with angels called friends, and robots like Rosie, to lend a hand. And when we all work together; we lift one another's burdens. And as for the rest we desperately desire, well God offers rest too.

Then Jesus said, "Come to me, all of you who are weary and carry heavy burdens, and I will give you rest. Take my yoke upon you. Let me teach you, because I am humble and gentle at heart, and you will find rest for your souls. For my yoke is easy to bear, and the burden I give you is light." (Matthew 11:28-30)

Hair Style

About two or three times a year I desire a new hair style. My thin and fine hair limits my styles, but I never give up hope. Staceymarie is my hairstylist and does a great job with my hair. She knows how to cut it just right and when she styles it, it looks different, great and beautiful. When I return home, I have the same old hair style. The problem isn't the cut, the problem is me, the stylist.

At my last appointment, I asked Staceymarie the question she probably dreads, "Can you do anything different with my hair?" She explained a few options on how I could style it differently. Then she said the words I dread, "curling iron." Given the choice between using a curling iron every day and my current hair style, I will keep the hair style. I just don't have the desire to spend a lot of time on my hair. On special occasions, I will spend some extra time, but for day to day adventures, this is as good as it gets.

We can look at our spiritual lives in the same manner as a new hair style. We can desire a new look, a deeper relationship with Christ. It can be major like a new area of ministry, or a gradual change where we build a deeper bond with Christ through Bible study. Perhaps we simply need to be still in God's presence and listen. Like my hair style, success in your new spiritual journey depends on the amount of time and work you devote to the changes. By no means does it take good works for salvation, but it does take hard work to grow as a Christian.

When the disciples chose to follow Jesus, they were aware of the effort ahead of them. In those days, if you were chosen to follow a Rabbi, you were committed to learn from him. In this case, Jesus selected hard-working laborers to follow Him. They had much to learn, but they were committed to the task. *(Mark 1:16-20)*. Ultimately, it was through these disciples the early church was founded. They no longer threw nets to catch fish. They threw nets to pull people out of their despair, and point them to the Savior.

Among these disciples was Simon, who Jesus later renamed Peter, the Rock. *(Matthew 16:18)*. In spite of all of Peter's biblical knowledge, he still had his ups and downs as a disciple. He was the only disciple with enough faith to walk on water—a definite high moment in his life. *(Matthew 14:27-33)*. Yet this same faith driven man hit a definitive low when he denied Christ three times. *(Matthew 26:69-75)*.

What gave Peter the strength to swing the pendulum so far and come out on top again? His hard work. His knowledge of the scriptures. His time spent with Jesus and the wisdom he gained. He committed himself to three years of the Rabbi's teachings, and was one of His closest followers. When life became difficult, he was able to recall the knowledge and lessons he learned along the way. When Christ changed Simon's name to Peter, He knew Peter would be the one who could stand strong in his faith, and start the first church. *(Acts 2)*.

Ironically, while I write this devotion, I received a new book review on my first devotional, *Bloom Where You're Planted*. Overall it was a great review and I thanked the reader for her input. Unfortunately, she was disappointed because I didn't encourage my readers to dive into the Word of God. For this reason, I only provided references today.

My own personal growth is directly related to my research and study in God's Word. As you read each devotion turn on the curling iron! In other words, heat up the intensity of your time with God each day. I encourage you to dig into God's Word. Not to be a better Christian, but to be a Christian who continually grows.

Personal Growth Challenges

- Don't just read God's Word, study the Word and apply it to your life.
- Consider using a prayer journal and increase your prayer life.
- Start a new ministry, or commit a time each week to a ministry at your church.
- Memorize a new scripture each week.
- Spend a quiet time with the Lord and meditate on a Bible verse.

"If I truly love Christ, I need to love the church as I would love Christ." (Quote from devotion, "Bridges of Love") We often relate to Peter throughout our daily struggles in life. Learn more about Peter's faith journey and his love for the church through devotions selected from *Bloom Where You're Planted*. Download your free devotion bundle, **Lessons from Peter**, at www.MaryRodman.com/BookBonuses.

Bathroom Remodel

You can learn a lot about yourself, your house, and others when you decide to remodel a room in your home. Your life is interrupted in some way, shape or form throughout the project, which causes stress and the tension rises. Your vision is different from your spouse's vision. We added a carpenter to the mix and based on what was feasible, his vision was slightly different from ours.

Our current remodeling project is the master bathroom. As the construction began you could say life turned into a new normal at the Rodman household. We are blessed with another full bathroom so we aren't to inconvenienced. It doesn't have much storage so we are living out of boxes on our dining room floor for the uncommon bathroom supplies, such as antacids. After a couple of weeks into the project I can stand in front of the boxes and find exactly what I need. (Well most of the time.)

At times, it seems like there is nothing normal about the project at all. Oh my, dirt and dust are everywhere. We were out of town when destruction began. Upon our return, it looked like the 1930's dust storm had blown through our home. In our haste to leave we never shut other doors to contain the mess. Commence melt down number one of the project! In my frustration, I began to clean.

I did the physical cleaning but not the cleansing of my heart. *"You were cleansed from your sins when you obeyed the truth, so now you must show sincere love to each other as brothers and sisters. Love each other deeply with all your heart." (1 Peter 1:22).* I did not feel much love toward my husband who insisted that we be out of town during the destruction phase. If I had been present a lot of work could have been prevented.

My next melt down of the project was over the cabinets. We salvaged part of the old cabinets and the carpenter made a new linen closet, medicine cabinet, and light fixture to match. When the new pieces arrived, they were more beautiful than the old. All I could see was the old ugly cabinets which did not match the new beautiful ones. It seemed like we had made a huge mistake. Our carpenter came to our rescue. He sanded, cleaned, and preformed other miracles on the old cabinets until they looked as good as the new ones.

Just as our carpenter cleaned the cabinets, Christ offers to cleanse us from our sins. In an ever so mysterious way, we begin to understand our need for a Savior and experience the Holy Spirit in our lives. It is the Holy Spirit who convicted me of my attitude throughout the project, and cleansed me.

> *But—When God our Savior revealed his kindness and love, he saved us, not because of the righteous things we had done, but because of his mercy. He washed away our sins, giving us a new birth and new life through the Holy Spirit. He generously poured out the Spirit upon us through Jesus Christ our Savior. (Titus 3:4-6)*

I quickly understood my heart needed to be cleansed after the cabinet miracle. I began to take on more of a "whatever" attitude about the project. It seemed to ease my stress and I no longer searched for the antacids (in the boxes on the floor) quite as often.

My reality check helped me understand that no wall is ever perfectly straight. No measurement exact. Not every tile will be placed precisely even on the floor, and no paint job is flawless. Will my bathroom remodel project be on a DIY Network show? No, but it serves its purpose. We gained storage space and a bigger shower.

The glass shower doors arrived today and the bathroom is now complete. All of the supplies have been returned to the bathroom and a new normal will begin as we search for items at their new locations.

Our memories are a strange gift from God. A month from now, I won't remember which box on the dining room floor contained my antacids. A year from now, I won't remember the little remodeling problems or why I let the small issues upset me. But I will remember I am blessed to have a remodeled bathroom. I pray every drop of water from my new rain shower head will remind me Christ washes away my sins. Even my sins of anger toward Jim, perfectionism on the project, and coveting the beautiful bathrooms on the DIY Network.

Life Is a Journey

Life is a journey we all have to take.
Often with pleasures and frequent mistakes.

Forgiveness is crucial to life's great demands.
But Christ offers grace with outstretched hands.

Come experience His grace and give Him your sins.
Through a childlike faith which comes from within.

He offers us life so abundant and free.
Please come to the altar upon bended knee.

With arms wide open Christ offers His grace.
He smiles and wipes the tears from your face.

Your freedom is found at the foot of the cross.
Because Jesus has given your sins a great toss.

The angels rejoice when a sinner's set free.
Praising and singing with angelic-like glee.

Thank you, dear Jesus for your love so amazing.
Now I'm rejoicing and constantly praising.

Oh, you who've never experienced the gain.
Won't you too let Jesus free you from stain?

Does He Notice?

Several months ago, I purchased a decorative two-tier wire basket for our kitchen. My plan was to put it under the kitchen counter but after I put it together it was too tall. Due to the business of life I brushed aside the idea and set it on the dining room table. It was there so long I am embarrassed to say receipts and knickknacks accumulated in the basket.

Eventually I tackled the cluttered table and moved items to their appropriate places. While cleaning up I realized the basket would fit behind my corner kitchen sink and I was very excited. I even found a couple of decorative cloth napkins to add a little color. The top basket contains potpourri and the bottom holds my dish soap, scratchers, sponges and such. It was the perfect location and cleaned the clutter from behind the sink.

At least two weeks passed before my husband, Jim, noticed the basket behind the sink. Granted Jim doesn't do the dishes but I'm sure it wasn't his first trip to the sink either. I thought to myself, "You didn't notice?" In Jim's defense, many times new tools or equipment appear in the barn and I don't notice them either. It is all in a person's perspective. You will always notice what is important to you.

The great news is we are all important to God, therefore He notices us. You are the person God sees and He cares for you deeply. As it says in *Isaiah 62:4b, "The Lord delights in you."*

No matter what your ups and downs are in life He chose you. Regardless of your past, in spite of your present, or how rocky your walk with Christ is, He still chose you. No experience in your life, no struggle, no joy, no blessing, no sadness was a mistake. He wanted you to experience all those parts of your life, because He chose you. The Bible tells us, *"Don't be afraid for I* am with you. Don't be discouraged for I am your God. I will strengthen you and help you. I will hold you up with my victorious right hand." (Isaiah 41:10).

Not only are you chosen by God but you are precious to Him. *Psalm 139* describes how uniquely God created each of us, but I love this verse. *"How precious are your thoughts about me, O God. They cannot be numbered!" (Psalm 139:17).*

As adults, we see little children as cute, fun loving, adorable, and precious. But when bad choices are made in life we tend to label ourselves and others as unworthy, unclean, and unacceptable. God doesn't label us. No matter our faults, our past, or our sins, we are all precious in His sight. We are all God's children.

You are chosen and precious but you are also a beloved child of God. *"See how much our Father loves us, for He calls us His children, and that is what we are!" (1 John 3:1a).* Each of us no matter our flaws are God's children and as God's children we are His royalty. *"Since we are his children, we are his heirs. In fact, together with Christ we are heirs of God's glory. But if we are to share his glory, we must also share his suffering." (Romans 8:17).*

Jim may have taken two weeks to see the basket behind the sink but God sees your every move. He is there at the exact moment when you need Him the most. He sees your struggles, your pain, your joy and your compassion.

"I will be faithful to you and make you mine, and you will finally know me as the Lord." (Hosea 2:20). God desires a loving relationship with you, His child, who He chose. You are precious in His sight. You are His beloved child. His royalty. If God had to do it all over again, He would change nothing about you. He loves all of your idiosyncrasies, your faults, your flaws, your past, your present, your beauty, your intelligence, and your smile.

My prayer for you today is that you understand and believe you are chosen. You are precious. You are His beloved child. You are royalty to the Almighty King.

Suggested Scripture Reading
- *Psalm 139:13-18*
- *Romans 8:15-17*
- *Psalm 72:12-14*

Partnership

One of my mother-in-law's famous quotes was, "Many hands make for light work." She would often say this to her grandchildren to enlist a little help. She could get them to do chores and they didn't realize they were working. After all, it is never considered work if Grandma makes life fun. Even though Leah has been gone many years, her famous quote lives on in our household.

Now that our bathroom remodel project is complete, I need to clean. (It truly amazes me how far drywall dust can travel!) House cleaning is also not my favorite pastime, but it is necessary at the moment. Thankfully I am not completing the task alone. Rosie and Reba are there to help. You were introduced to Rosie in an earlier devotion, and Reba is my favorite country musician, who recently released a Christian album. On day two, we formed a partnership to get the job done. After all, "Many hands make for light work."

They weren't the hands Leah referred to, but it did help. I wiped windows, walls and baseboards, Rosie cleaned the floors, and Reba sang. It lifted my spirit to sing praise music while I worked. My attitude went from, ugh another room to clean, to one of joy as I sang along. My new attitude stayed with me in the days to come, as I thoroughly cleaned each room. I loved my new work partnership, but I have to give credit where credit is due. It wasn't the partnership with Rosie and Reba which made the difference in my attitude, it was Jesus. You will automatically partner with Jesus through any undesirable situation when you sing words like:

> *Hallelujah for the heartache.*
> *Hallelujah for the good days.*
> *Hallelujah for every breath we get.*
> *Hallelujah Amen.*[v]

We often look to Jesus on our difficult days. Those times when we feel like our whole world has crumbled beneath our feet. The reality is Jesus is in our everyday lives as well. Those day to day dreaded chores. Your sleepless nights. Your loneliness. Your chaos. Your work. Your joys. Your heartaches. No matter what turmoil your day brings, He is with you.

The Bible mentions women (two of them by name) who worked in the background to support Jesus' ministry. We know little about these ladies, but we can still learn from them. *"Joanna, the wife of Chuza, Herod's business manager; Susanna; and many others who were contributing from their own resources to support Jesus and his disciples." (Luke 8:3).* It was unusual for women to follow a rabbi in biblical times, yet Jesus allowed these ladies to follow Him. I guess you could say, Jesus was one of the first equal opportunity employers.

These ladies had demons cast out of them and experienced physical healings. No doubt they felt a great deal of gratitude toward Christ. Yet they worked behind the scenes and helped support Him financially. They didn't tell their stories to an audience of people. They were the ones who quietly served where few people noticed. You know this type of person. The one who sets up, and cleans up at events. These ladies probably cooked and cleaned and even did the dishes and the laundry while others spread the Good News.

These quiet servants of Jesus, like Susanna and Joanna, had chores they probably dreaded, some sleepless nights, and chaotic days. But they partnered with Christ, as they relied on Him to direct their steps. Christ provided joy throughout the mundane tasks in life. He even made the mundane seem glorious.

We also need to praise Jesus in the mundane, dreaded duties of life, and allow Him to lift our spirits. These ladies understood how important Christ was in all situations. No matter the work at hand or the cost involved, they continually followed Jesus. In the end, these ladies were rewarded for their faithfulness. They were blessed to be the first at the tomb on Easter morning. They were privileged to tell the apostles that Christ had risen! What a great reward from Christ for their daily, mundane, behind the scenes devotion to His ministry. *(Luke 24)*.

So how about you? Will you form a partnership with Christ to complete the dreaded chores in life with joy? I highly recommend it because the rewards are out of this world!

Suggested Scripture Reading
- *Luke 8:1-3*
- *Luke 24:1-12*

Ground Sparrow

I absolutely love when God paints a real-life picture of scripture. This section of scripture is familiar to me, but not one I often dwell upon.

> *What is the price of five sparrows—two copper coins? Yet God does not forget a single one of them. And the very hairs on your head are all numbered. So don't be afraid; you are more valuable to God than a whole flock of sparrows. I tell you the truth, everyone who acknowledges me publicly here on earth, the Son of Man will also acknowledge in the presence of God's angels. (Luke 12:6-8)*

While I trimmed bushes earlier this week the small ground sparrows went crazy. They flew around and sang up a storm. They definitely wanted my attention but I continued to work on the bushes. Eventually I came upon the source of their disturbance. Nestled in the center of a bush were two tiny nests. There were no eggs or babies so I wondered why they were so upset with me. I quickly cut around the nests, finished, and left.

Later in the afternoon I went outside to water the flower basket, and they were still fluttering around acting crazy. I discovered the true source of their excitement; a baby sparrow had left the nest and was perched in the grass. I realized the birds were using their God given instincts to protect their baby, not concerned about their nests. We too were given instincts to protect ourselves but our protection and comfort come from the Holy Spirit.

God cares deeply for us and knows everything about us. When we acknowledge Him publicly, Christ acknowledges us in the presence of His angels! As I watched the birds fluttering to protect the baby sparrow in the grass, it was like a picture of the angels watching over you and me. This vision of God's love and shield around me brought great comfort.

It was as if the birds were saying, "Here's my child who I will protect."

The Son of Man said to His angels, "Here's my child who I will protect."

When I searched the word *sparrow* in the Bible, I found more references than I expected. I was searching for the scripture above which can be found in both *Matthew* and *Luke*. But I also found these beautiful words below.

The baby sparrow probably longed to return to the nest for refuge from a scary world. We as Christians long for the same—refuge in the presence of the Son of Man. And today, as I write this story, I am desperately seeking refuge under His wings. God's timing is amazing. His Bible stories are ageless. His refuge is like no other. Join the baby sparrow and me—fly home and rest in the presence of the Son of Man today.

> *How lovely is your dwelling place,*
> *O Lord of Heaven's Armies.*
> *I long, yes, I faint with longing*
> *to enter the courts of the Lord.*
> *With my whole being, body and soul,*
> *I will shout joyfully to the living God.*
> *Even the sparrow finds a home,*
> *and the swallow builds her nest and raises her young*
> *at a place near your altar,*
> *O Lord of Heaven's Armies, my King and my God!*
> *What joy for those who can live in your house,*
> *always singing your praises.*
> *(Psalm 84:1-4)*

Generations

Jim and I built a float to salute my Dad for our local 4th of July parade. The theme was *Small Town Memories* and Dad has been a part of the community for most of his life. He is a WWII veteran who served in the navy. He loves his family, his community and his country. Our float theme was *Memories Bloom for Generations*, and it was centered around the four generations who rode on the float. Dad, myself and Jim (our driver), our sons and their wives, and our 3.9 grandchildren. (Kim is due with our fourth grandchild any day.) We are just a small part of Dad's family but we had a great time as we waved to family and friends.

We are proud of our four generations. Dad's immediate family including spouses, range in age from two to ninety. Sadly, five loved ones have gone on to be with the Lord. We are thirty-six strong and the baby will soon make thirty-seven. As you can imagine with a large family we sometimes bicker and squabble but we also rally around when times are difficult.

My dad loves the grandchildren and the great-grandchildren as *Proverbs 17:6* resonates in his life. *"Grandchildren are the crowning glory of the aged; parents are the pride of their children."* Dad set the bar high when we were growing up. Not with words but by example. He was a church going, God fearing, hard-working man, who expected the same from his children.

You can find examples of genealogy throughout the New and Old Testaments. Sections like *Ruth 4:18-22* which shows the Moabite Ruth as part of the lineage of Christ. Matthew felt genealogy was important and listed all the generations from Abraham to Jesus in *Matthew 1*. Throughout the generations there were times of idol worship as they turned from God. For example,

"During Rehoboam's reign, the people of Judah did what was evil in the Lord's sight, provoking his anger with their sin, for it was even worse than that of their ancestors." (1 Kings 14:22). Yet woven among the evil there were always glimpses of leaders who were—church going, God fearing, hard-working men.

I was blessed with this type of leader in my home, unlike many who are not. You often read or hear about generational curses. This simply means that from generation to generation you repeat the sins of your ancestors. This can be any type of sin. We categorize the sins but God does not. It can be addictions, abuse, idol worship, or witchcraft. But it is also coveting, lying, slander, gossip, and keeping a day of rest. Often it is those hidden generational sins which go unnoticed and still have an impact on the family.

But there is good news. Every time the Israelites turned back to God the Lord rescued them. (*Judges 3:9) (1 Samuel 12:10-11).* If you have a generational sin in your family God will do the same for you. When you repent, Christ will make you a new creation. *(2 Corinthians 5:17).*

> *And so, dear brothers and sisters, I plead with you to give your bodies to God because of all he has done for you. Let them be a living and holy sacrifice—the kind he will find acceptable. This is truly the way to worship him. Don't copy the behavior and customs of this world, but let God transform you into a new person by changing the way you think. Then you will learn to know God's will for you, which is good and pleasing and perfect. (Romans 12:1-2)*

Let the change in your family begin with you. Don't allow a generational curse begin with you either. If you were raised by a church going, God fearing, hard-working man, and have drifted away from the Lord return and ask for forgiveness. The example you set today will pave a path for future generations so break the chains of a generational curse.

Dad on the float for the parade, July 4, 2017

Sad Memory

Not long ago I heard a song which was a flash from my past. It had been years since I had actually listened to the words and it brought back sad memories for me. They were difficult days and dark times as I made tough decisions in my life. I was in a failing marriage and felt trapped. As I look back, I can see how God was with me, but in those darkest days I was far from Him. I relied on the words to a song which truly offered no comfort.

As I listened to the words, "Here I go again on my own. Like a drifter, I was born to walk alone[vi]." I was saddened by my mindset of so long ago and shocked I ever felt so lonely. I have grown in my faith and now understand I am never alone! My outlook on life would have been so different had I understood God's love for me on those dark days. Yet somewhere deep in my soul, I believe I did know because the divorce and the lonely times are exactly what lead me back to Christ. When you and I face dark days, we can read of God's wonderful promises.

> *And the Lord himself, the King of Israel, will live among you! At last your trouble will be over, and you will never again fear disaster. On that day the announcement to Jerusalem will be. "Cheer up, Zion! Don't be afraid! For the Lord your God is living among you. He is a mighty savior. He will take delight in you with gladness. With his love, he will calm all your fears. He will rejoice over you with joyful songs." (Zephaniah 3:15b-17)*

If I had read these words years ago, hopefully I would have found comfort in the Lord instead of feeling like a lonely drifter. I am so thankful God pulled me out of the darkness! I now rejoice with words of hope such as *Psalm 70:4, "But may all who search for you be filled with joy and gladness in you. May those who love your salvation repeatedly shout, 'God is Great!'"*

If you feel like a drifter, I pray you find comfort in the Word of the Lord. Christ too felt lonely and abandoned as He hung on the cross. *(Mark 15:34)*. But because of His sacrifice on the cross we will never walk alone. The Holy Spirit is His gift to us. He will always be our Comforter. *(Acts 2:38)*.

Below are the words often spoken prior to communion. They are also words which comfort those who feel lonely. As you read the account of the first communion, notice there was a second cup of wine. It symbolizes the new covenant with Christ. There was no longer a need for the Old Testament sacrifices for the atonement of our sins. Christ was the perfect sacrifice for all eternity. When you put your faith in Him, you will never walk alone!

> *Then he took a cup of wine and gave thanks to God for it. Then he said, "Take this and share it among yourselves. For I will not drink wine again until the Kingdom of God has come." He took some bread and gave thanks to God for it. Then he broke it in pieces and gave it to the disciples, saying, "This is my body, which is given for you. Do this in remembrance of me."* **After supper he took another cup of wine and said, "This cup is the new covenant between God and his people— an agreement confirmed with my blood, which is poured out as a sacrifice for you.** *(Luke 22:17-20 - Emphasis added)*

Get Out of Your Box

A couple of months ago my granddaughters had great fun as they played in a plastic tub. Reagan was so tiny she was able to curl up inside. Mya started to put the lid over her but we of course told her no. I snapped a picture as they played and it is one of our favorite photos of the girls.

Just last week Reagan said over and over again, "I want to play that." For the life of me I could not figure out what *that* was. I finally asked her to show me and she took me to the picture of her in the plastic tub. She obviously enjoyed the moment and the picture was a great reminder of a fun day. Unfortunately, it has been filled with items and put away so she wasn't able to play again. But Grandpa was quick to tell me to purchase them a new tub for future playtimes.

When I look at the picture of Reagan in the plastic tub more comes to mind than just the girls playing. Mya and Reagan laughed, giggled and enjoyed life. But we often crawl in our tub or our box to hide. We refuse to allow ourselves to enjoy life and we stay in our box. Worse yet sometimes we even decide to close the lid and vow to never come out!

God has great plans for our lives but we need to take refuge under His wings not in a box. *(Psalm 91:4)*. Please heed the advice of someone who used to live in her box with the lid on and closed tight. Life is meant to be lived! Yes, there may be times of failure, embarrassment, and discouragement. You may shed a tear. You may shake your fist at God in anger. But please remove the lid from your box and seek shelter from the Most High as you soar. You will find an abundant life. A life greater than you ever imagined. Wonderful opportunities are in store for those who come out of their box to live for Christ.

*Those who live in the shelter of the Most High
will find rest in the shadow of the Almighty.
This I declare about the Lord:
He alone is my refuge, my place of safety;
he is my God, and I trust him.
(Psalm 91:1-2)*

Suggested Scripture Reading
- Psalm 91

Mya and Reagan playing with the plastic tub.

Be Strong and Immovable

So, my dear brothers and sisters, be strong and immovable. Always work enthusiastically for the Lord, for you know that nothing you do for the Lord is ever useless. (1 Corinthians 15:58)

I looked at my list of possible devotions and began to search the scriptures to accompany the story I was about to write. Instead, this little gem from *1 Corinthians* piqued my interest so I set aside all of my other thoughts and plans.

Jim and I have the privilege of hosting a wonderful missionary family who are coming to Ohio to share the gospel. Yesterday I contacted various churches in the vicinity about the opportunity to be a host church, but none were interested. I posted about them on social media, but no one expressed interest or even commented. I plan to make more phone calls today but I am afraid of more rejection.

Our plan is to find venues or churches for them to speak Friday through Sunday. Of course, Sunday was easy to fill because as a society we typically attend church on Sunday. The discouragement comes from the lack of interest churches have to share the gospel on the other days. Many churches wouldn't entertain the idea of a Friday or Saturday event. As a result, I have thrown in the towel due to frustration. I developed a why bother attitude. If no one else seems to care about the impact their testimony may have on others, why should I.

It is sad to hear pastors make comments such as:
"No one in this church will come out on a week night."

"Friday or Saturday, no way can we draw a crowd."

"My congregation won't even attend a Good Friday service, so why would they come to this."

What has happened in our churches today? Do we warm the pews on Sunday morning and forget to share the gospel the rest of the week? Our responsibility to share the gospel is more than Sunday morning church services.

As a society, we see less and less commitment everywhere. Not just commitment to the church and the gospel but commitment to serve and reach out with personal contact. We live in a world of text messages and social media and we are losing personal contact. I'm not criticizing the social media trend. I use it as an outreach tool myself. But it has allowed us to become detached and uninvolved when it pertains to sharing the gospel of Christ in our local community. We need to focus back on *1 Corinthians 15:58* and be strong and immoveable because our work for Christ is never wasted. In this case, a personal touch can be the difference between heaven or hell for an eternity. Maybe I'm a dreamer or some would say I'm forever the optimist, but this is how I see it.

> If one church will host the missionaries on Friday night.
>
> And if one member of this church invites one person to hear the gospel.
>
> And if that one person's heart is touched by the missionary's testimony, one soul will be saved.
>
> When one soul is saved, angels rejoice in heaven.
>
> And so the cycle continues, when that one new Christian reaches another.

I know, there are a lot of ifs, but all those ifs bathed in prayer will change lives. It isn't a lack of commitment it is a lack of concern for others and where they may spend eternity!

As the verse says, be strong, immovable and enthusiastic when you work for the Lord. Take the time to make a difference in someone's life today. Someone's eternity may depend on your actions.

As for me, I have phone calls to make today. I pray I can find one church, with one member, who will invite one person to church on a Friday or Saturday night to hear the gospel.

Long-Distance Friends

I recently became friends with Leah as a result of my first book. We have never met in person. I live in Ohio and she lives in New York. I read her blogs and am inspired by her strong faith through many struggles in her life. Regardless of these battles she is always focused on Christ and His goodness.

She currently is recuperating from some back problems but she also has a rare bone disease. Her mom's cancer has spread and her son has some special medical problems as well. You could easily say, she and her family have more than they can handle but not without the help of God! In spite of all these health issues her creativity continues to flow as she speaks words of encouragement through social media. She continually praises God with all of her heart, mind, and soul.

Today God urged me to pray for Leah. I obviously can't go give her a big girlfriend hug two states away, but I can pray. I asked God to give her comfort and peace. How much more can my long-distance friend possibly endure when her burdens are so heavy at times? I later learned her aunt had passed away and they were traveling to her funeral about an hour away. No wonder she needed my prayers. It would be a long emotional day for her so I prayed again only with more specific prayers. I asked God to give her the necessary strength for the funeral and for their safe travels.

As I ponder this blooming long-distance friendship, I find it is centered around some wonderful verses found in *1 Thessalonians 5*.

"Rejoice always." No matter what Leah or myself face in life we always rejoice in the Lord! We are able to face our struggles with great joy because God also blesses our lives.

"Pray without ceasing." From the funeral to her medical problems, Leah is always in my prayers. What a privilege and gift from God to stand in the gap as a prayer warrior for her and others.

Our lives will continue to have ups and downs because that is just life. Regardless, we will remember *"in everything give thanks; for this is the will of God in Christ Jesus for you."* It's not always easy to give thanks for the problems and struggles in life but those battles produce a stronger faith as we cling tightly to Christ.

Today was a perfect example of the last verse, *"Do not quench the Spirit."* I felt the urge to pray for Leah and obediently did so. I did not know of her loss when I first began to pray. I simply lifted her to the Lord. You will receive wonderful blessings when you listen to the Holy Spirit and pray for others.

I prayed for my long-distance friend today but Jesus taught me much more. The scriptures came to life which always brings me great joy. In the future, when I chat on-line with Leah or say a prayer for her I will remember this wonderful scripture. What a perfect example of these precious words God gave me through our long-distance friendship.

> *Rejoice always, pray without ceasing, in everything give thanks; for this is the will of God in Christ Jesus for you. Do not quench the Spirit. (1 Thessalonians 5:16-19 NKJV)*

Rejoice in the ups and downs of life. Pray continually for those around you. Be thankful through both your struggles and your joys. Always seek God's will and listen to the Holy Spirit. What wonderful words of wisdom in these few short verses! As you reflect on this scripture allow the Holy Spirit to lead you throughout your day and in your prayers.

Why Me Lord?

Some days you want to throw your hands in the air and say, "Why me Lord?" Today is one of those days for Jim, or actually one of those summers. We bale tons of straw (literally) on the farm for resale. Some years we fill the barn in about three weeks, but this year we aren't so lucky. For every good sunny day to bale straw we have five or six days of rain or damp weather. With each rain the quality of the straw decreases and the decisions get harder. Each morning Jim has to decide—do we bale today or try to let it dry more praying the rain holds off? Needless to say, Jim has been discouraged and his stress level has been high.

Our main customer for the straw is a dairy farm. The straw is mixed with food rations for the cows so they use only top-quality straw. In an attempt to sell some of the poor-quality straw Jim and his partner, Stan, decided to take a load to an auction in Amish country this week. On day one, they drove about three miles and the truck broke down. No worries they can go to a different Amish auction tomorrow. Jim borrowed a truck and off they went again. They lost money on the load of straw! They had more invested in the load of straw than the buyer paid. Believe it or not, their day got even worse.

The buyer gave them horrible directions to his farm to unload the straw. They were lost (though men never admit they are truly lost) and ran out of diesel fuel on the way. In total frustration Jim called for me to bring them diesel fuel. He was headed uphill when he ran out of fuel. There he sat frustrated with his foot on the brakes to prevent rolling backwards and jackknifing. Just as he called God sent two angels to their rescue. They brought some diesel fuel and they even knew where the farm was located. Amen and thank you Jesus!

If you're not a farmwife you might find it difficult to relate to this story, but we all have struggles in life. There are days when we throw our hands in the air and say, "Why me Lord? What did I do to deserve this?" We know our Christian life isn't always easy and neither was Job's life.

God allowed Job to lose all of his possessions and even his family. His friends pop in for a visit and rather than providing comfort they accuse him of wrongdoing. They claim God is punishing him for some hidden sins. Job argues he is innocent, and refuses to repent. His wife doesn't treat him much better. She told him to *"curse God and die"* but Job refused. *(Job 2:9b)*. (Now granted I didn't want to rescue Jim today, but I would have in a heartbeat. Absolutely no way would I speak those words to him.)

Jim has faced some difficult days but it doesn't mean God has abandoned him. He is a sovereign and just God. His ways are beyond our understanding. We cannot fathom His omnipotence. We may never know—who, what, when, where or why—but we can take a step of faith and trust in His sovereignty.

Throughout the story, Job continually questions God. Where are you God? Why are you treating me this way God? *(Job 30:20-21)*. Job's friends continually plead with him to repent and ironically in the final chapter he does. But he doesn't repent of some secret sin, he asks forgiveness for his lack of trust in God. Job had questioned God's sovereignty and justice. Ultimately, he humbled himself before the Lord and admitted he had no right to question God Almighty.

Don't allow the sin of "Why me Lord?" cloud your days and your relationship with God. We will never totally understand our omnipotent Father. However, we can put our doubts aside and trust in the Everlasting Father and His sovereign ways. May you draw closer to God and His power today as you read Job's prayer of repentance.

Then Job replied to the Lord:
"I know that you can do anything,
and no one can stop you.
You asked, 'Who is this that questions my
wisdom with such ignorance?'
It is I—and I was talking about things I knew
nothing about,
things far too wonderful for me.
You said, 'Listen and I will speak!
I have some questions for you,
and you must answer them.'
I had only heard about you before,
but now I have seen you with my own eyes.
I take back everything I said,
and I sit in dust and ashes to show my
repentance."
(Job 42:1-6)

The Cleaver Family

Today I watched an episode of the old show *Leave It to Beaver*. Don't we all wish our world was as wonderful and happy as it was for the Cleaver family? No matter what trouble the Beaver got into all was good at the end of the day. Occasionally Wally was your typical teenager but he always looked out for Beaver and took his role as a big brother seriously. Ward used what I refer to as book-end punishment. Love, discipline, and more love. Punishment was never argued about and was always received with a "Yes sir." And what about June? I'm glad I don't have to wear a dress in the kitchen but she was the model wife and mother. Dinner was always on the table. Groceries in the cupboard. A kiss and a hug to Ward each morning. Rooms were clean. Hair was perfect. I honestly think she was the Proverbs 31 woman.

If you watch the show often you begin to wonder what happened to this world? Did a family like the Cleaver's exist or was it only in Hollywood? I'm sure it is a little bit of both. Times have definitely changed since the 1950's when the show was filmed. Fewer stay-at-home moms and more single parent families. Fewer outdoor activities with other children and more iPads, computers and alone time. But the change which has impacted society the most is the lack of Christian values taught in the home. It is difficult during those child rearing years to be a model family like the Cleavers.

Country artist Reba McEntire recently recorded a Christian song titled, "Back to God." The lyrics say we should give this world back to God in prayer. Maybe the Cleaver family had it right. Maybe at the end of the day they were on their knees as they gave all their problems, anger, and frustrations back to

God. In order for us to give this world back to God we need to return Christian values in our homes.

Values such as worshipping God and respect for others. Jesus commands this of us. *"And you must love the Lord your God with all your heart, all your soul, all your mind and all your strength. The second is equally important: Love your neighbor as yourself. No other commandment is greater than these." (Mark 12:30-31).*

Humility and honesty. I believe the Cleaver family displayed these values and instilled them in their children. Even though Wally or Beaver would get in trouble, they were humble, considerate and honest about their faults. *"Pride leads to disgrace, but with humility comes wisdom. Honesty guides good people; dishonesty destroys treacherous people." (Proverbs 11:2-3).*

Forgiveness and Generosity. Not just the forgiveness for one another as it says in *Colossians 3:12-14*. Forgiveness begins when we understand and accept God's mercy for our own sins. When you make Christ the Lord of your life you begin to show others more forgiveness. Soon generosity will follow as you become generous with your time, resources, talents, and money.

If you aren't familiar with the Cleaver Family, I hope you can enjoy an episode of the old TV show. No matter your choice of episodes you will find a Christian value you wish was more prevalent in your own home. Take time to learn from the Cleavers and give your problems, anger, and frustrations back to God. Strive to make the changes in your own home, which you would like to see in our world. Remember change in your home, will bring change to your community. Change in your community, will bring change in our country. And change in our country, will bring change in our world.

Person to person, moment to moment, as we love, we change the world.
~ Samahria Lyte Kaufman[vii]

Rotisserie

Sometimes in life we walk through processes which we simply do not enjoy. My most recent experience was a sleep apnea test. If you have not experienced one, I pray you never will. After completing the test, I wonder, has anyone ever been told they do not have a sleeping disorder? Think about it. How do you sleep in a strange bed with wires attached knowing someone is watching you?

I had wires attached to my head, my legs, and my chest. The ointment had a burning sensation for my overly sensitive skin, which started the cooking process. I crawled into a hard bed (way before my bedtime), which was covered with a plastic mattress pad cover. I don't do plastic or foam without sweating profusely. So, it was like someone put me in the oven to roast! I flipped and I flopped. I turned on the rotisserie all night until I was well done. I was so relieved when she woke me at 5:30 a.m. to send me home! You could say this turkey was well basted by morning. My pajamas were soaked from all of the sweat, and I was exhausted from the lack of sleep.

Some people don't report for a second day of testing. Nope, not me. I was one of the lucky ones who was told to return for a second night. A week later, I went through the same process again, but this time they added a CPAP machine. Wow—another joyful night's sleep! The same hot, hard bed. The same ointment and the same wires. But now I'm attached to a CPAP machine. I did sleep better than the first night, but throughout the rotisserie process I lost my air hose three times. I so desperately wanted some rest that I seriously considered using the air hose like a fan to cool myself rather than reattaching it to the CPAP machine. The test is now complete (Praise the Lord!) and I am waiting on the actual diagnosis. I believe however it is self-explanatory since they connected me to a CPAP machine.

Throughout both tests, I had a sweet technician by the name of Rachel. I was not the best patient, and I definitely had an attitude on day two. After all, who looks forward to being rewired and re-roasted? But Rachel was ever so kind and joyful. It would be a sacrifice for me to stay up all night and watch people sleep, but she chose this as her profession. Her only advantage—she didn't have to get wired and roasted. I pray my attitude was not too harsh and that I kept my tongue under control. The experience was not Rachel's fault, so there was no need to take my frustrations out on her.

We are warned about the wickedness of our tongues in James 3. *"The tongue is a small thing that makes grand speeches. But a tiny spark can set a great forest on fire. And among all the parts of the body, the tongue is a flame of fire. It is a whole world of wickedness, corrupting your entire body. It can set your whole life on fire, for it is set on fire by hell itself." (James 3:5-6).*

James goes on to say, we can tame animals, reptiles and birds, but we struggle with our own tongues. I know I never cursed at Rachel, but I presented an undertone of disdain for the process. Therefore, my words were not words of love and compassion when we chatted. I was definitely not a witness to all the wonderful blessings of Christ. I was just plain grumpy.

Our conversations can do one of two things. *"Sometimes it praises our Lord and Father, and sometimes it curses those who have been made in the image of God." (James 3:9).*

It was sweet Rachel who turned our conversation into praise. She shared how God provided her with the financial means to purchase a home. She had dreamed of owning her own home and was excited to share about her blessings. With excitement, she also shared about a friend who painted her cathedral ceilings and walls when she could not.

It was a humbling moment as God reminded me that He has also provided us with a beautiful home. Plus, a friend who painted our entire house, including a cathedral ceiling. My focus instantly changed from my rotisserie experience to my blessed life.

Blessings come in all areas of our lives, even roasting at the sleep clinic. It proved to me that God is present in all situations. As a result, when the next dreaded process comes my way, this turkey hopes to turn up the heat and enjoy the rotisserie. I pray God reminds me to rewire my attitude and my tongue so I can praise Jesus in all circumstances.

Sweet Aroma

I love to take a morning walk as the sun rises and the air is cool. But today the fog would not lift. I longed for a quiet walk with Jesus and decided to make the best of the situation as I walked up and down our long driveway a couple of times. I was disappointed in my scenery because of the fog. There was no inspirational sunrise, simply corn, corn and more corn. But it wasn't long until I realized God had a plan.

I began to pray for some friends and family who truly need God's healing and presence in their lives. Then my prayers changed to my lack of ideas for devotions. As I poured out my frustrations to the Lord, I began to notice the aroma of the corn. I love the smell of corn as it grows. The scent is strongest during pollination but today's damp August air made it very aromatic. My first thought was my allergies and how a walk surrounded by corn might be a bad idea. But then God reminded me of these words found in the scriptures. *"A pleasing aroma to the Lord."*

When you do a Bible search on those exact words in the New Living Translation of the Bible you will find approximately thirty-five references in the books of Exodus, Leviticus and Numbers. All of which refer to the sacrifices required by the old law for the atonement of sins. Many of them will say, *"A special gift presented to the Lord."* God liked the aroma of these sacrifices but it was more than the aroma which pleased Him. It was their repentant hearts which pleased Him most. Then Jesus came along and He changed everything! We no longer have to follow the Old Testament sacrifices. He laid down His life for the atonement of all our sins. *"He loved us and offered himself as a sacrifice for us, a pleasing aroma to God." (Ephesians 5:2b).*

To those who believe in Christ this journey is a sweet aroma. We put our faith in God and thank Him for supplying our daily needs. We follow Christ wherever He leads because we are called to be a witness of His greatness. We no longer offer the grain and animal sacrifices of the Old Testament; we present our lives to Christ as His servants.

Some people do not understand the glorious abundant life Christ offers. To them this story has a dreadful smell, instead of a sweet aroma. Since they don't understand they find reasons to deny the truth and walk away without understanding Christ's saving grace.

As Christ's servants, we are called to reach the lost and to live each day as a witness to Christ's greatness. Christ calls us to—Share the Truth. Lend a hand. Teach. Pray. Serve. Each of us has a story to tell or a favorite Bible verse to encourage others. We are called to be an example of Christ's love to all. *"We preach the word of God with sincerity and with Christ's authority, knowing that God is watching us." (2 Corinthians 2:17b).*

We are faced with a choice each day. Will we choose to be silent about the grace of Jesus or will we choose to make our lives a sweet aroma as we witness for Christ? Even on the difficult days, I rise each morning and decide to be a witness to God's glory. I pray you too will commit to following Christ and share your story just as David wrote, *"Come and listen, all you who fear God, and I will tell you what he did for me." (Psalm 66:16).*

Suggested Scripture Reading
- *2 Corinthians 2:14-17*
- *Psalm 66:16-20*
- *Matthew 28:18-20*

Garbage Dump

We live on a country road along the river. It is a beautiful drive from one end to the other. You see glimpses of the river as you wind around curves. To the south is a beautiful tunnel of trees and of course the occasional deer may cross your path. Unfortunately, people dump their trash along the river from time to time. In the last couple of weeks someone dumped numerous bags of trash and miscellaneous items which included a hot tub cover and a mattress! I was raised to not even throw a gum wrapper out a car window so I find this inexcusable. Why do they treat this beautiful road like a trash dumpster? Maybe they don't have the funds for the proper disposal of large items or simply they are disrespectful.

When trash is dumped, I find it much easier to properly dispose of my physical trash than I do my emotional garbage. Specifically, the emotion of anger. Anger about a situation can cause us to lash out at those we love when in actuality it isn't their fault. Jim and I have been guilty of this from time to time. But the more mature we get, the less it happens. I don't mean mature as in our age (which seems to grow exponentially) but more mature in Christ. The years of ups and downs, and the trials of life have increased our faith and taught us to focus on the big picture.

Let's look at the story of Sarai and Hagar in *Genesis 16*. God promised Abram and Sarai a son, yet many years later Sarai was still unable to bear children. Sarai didn't see this as any great surprise due to her age and took matters into her own hands. She did not trust God to provide a son through her and she gives her servant Hagar to Abram as a wife. Granted this was not an uncommon practice in Old Testament times but after Hagar becomes pregnant a quarrel ensues. They begin to treat one another with jealousy, disdain and contempt. I'm not surprised, are you? What was most likely a close friendship between a servant and master turned into jealousy and hatred for one another.

Sarai created this problem but she had no intentions of accepting the blame or the garbage it created. No doubt Hagar taunted her but Sarai dumps the blame entirely on Abram. *"Then Sarai said to Abram, 'This is all your fault! I put my servant into your arms, but now that she's pregnant she treats me with contempt. The Lord will show who's wrong—you or me!'" (Genesis 16:5).*

I want to stop in my tracks and say to Sarai, "Just wait one-minute missy! You caused this problem when you gave him another wife. How in the world can you blame Abram?" Abram obviously felt the same way because he throws it right back at her saying, *"Look, she is your servant, so deal with her as you see fit." (Genesis 16:6).* Abram sends a clear message to Sarai and he is wiping his hands of the entire situation.

Wow a marital fight right there in the Bible! Not to mention all of the misplaced anger in this story. Sarai is mad because she gave Hagar to Abram as his wife. Hagar is jealous and angry because even though she is pregnant she will always be second fiddle in the family. And Abram? Well he is just angry about the entire situation.

Anger is a natural emotion God gave us but He also tells us to control our anger. The book of Proverbs has many references about anger. Sarai, Hagar and Abram could have used some of Solomon's words of wisdom on the issue. We are fortunate to have the Bible for advice today. My favorite scripture about anger is found in *James*. It addresses the issue of selfish anger just like the story of Sarai and Hagar.

Understand this, my dear brothers and sisters: You must all be quick to listen, slow to speak, and slow to get angry. Human anger does not produce the righteousness God desires. So get rid of all the filth and evil in your lives, and humbly accept the word God has planted in your hearts, for it has the power to save your souls. (James 1:19-21)

My Christian maturity has taught me to be slow to anger and consider others before I lash out and point fingers. I pray I never set a bad Christian example by dumping my garbage on others. The lives we live, and the talk we talk, are the greatest witness we can give an unsaved world. So please don't dump your garbage in anger on a loved one, especially one who desperately needs a relationship with Christ.

Encouragement

Today as I left the pharmacy this lady runs out the door toward me. In her sweet southern Alabama drawl, she asked, "Are you Mary?"

"Yes," I said.

"Can I hug you?"

Leisa wrapped her arms around me and hugged me tight. She proceeded to tell me how much my book has helped her and her family members through difficult days. Her daddy recently passed away after a short illness and throughout his illness Leisa made many trips south to visit. She always left a copy of my book with family or friends as encouragement. Upon her return, she would purchase another copy for herself at the pharmacy which is exactly what she was doing today.

Leisa left the small pharmacy in such a hurry to speak with me she had not paid for her prescription. She began to worry so I quickly signed her devotional and we went inside to talk. The clerk smiled and reassured her everything was okay since she sent her to meet me.

Leisa said she doesn't read the devotional book in any sense of an order but opens it each morning and allows God to speak to her heart. God always takes her to a devotion which encourages her and gives her hope for the day. What a wonderful mighty God we serve. He can direct our steps and He can lead you to the perfect devotion in a book or the perfect scripture in your Bible. Leisa and I talked more, she hugged me again and we left.

We parted ways in a physical sense but not in a spiritual sense. She deeply touched my heart with encouragement and heartfelt love for my stories and devotions. As tears ran down my cheeks I hopped back in the truck and headed for home. Leisa wanted to thank me for the encouragement she found in my devotional book, but I want to go back and hug her again for the kind words she spoke to me.

In recent days, I have been overwhelmed with the marketing side of ministry. I have created marketing materials, spent time on social media and put my book into more local businesses. All of which overwhelms me. I don't want to be a marketing rep but it comes with my ministry. I would rather write and speak about God's grace, encourage others, and plant seeds of faith. Yet honestly, if I look back over my life God has blessed me with all the necessary marketing skills to accomplish the ministry He has given me.

I was ready to say, "It is enough Lord. I'm throwing in the towel. I can't do this anymore." And God sent an angel to bless me. Simply knowing my book touched one life, or encouraged one person through difficult days is all the encouragement I need to continue. I can sum up today's touching moment with Leisa by sharing one of my favorite Bible verses with you. *"When we get together, I want to encourage you in your faith, but I also want to be encouraged by yours." (Romans 1:12).*

O Lord, thank you for the many blessings I receive each day, especially those I take for granted. You continually love me and guard my heart even when I am unaware. When life is discouraging, You always lift me high in ways I cannot fathom.

Today when I was ready to say, "It is enough Lord, I can't continue to do all you ask of me," you sent an angel to light my way. Kind words of encouragement. Sincere hugs of compassion and caring. Words spoken by a true angel here on earth, who was a stranger until today.

Lord be with Leisa and all those encouragers that cross our paths daily. Father, lead me from this place of confusion with the heavy load ministry can sometimes bring. Let me trust in you and find new strength each day. Enable me to soar high on wings like eagles that I may continue to do Your work and encourage others with the words You give me to write and speak. Amen.

Fire of Blessings

Occasionally God allows our faith to be tested through the storms of life. In those moments, how will we react? Will we remember the Rock is our foundation? Or will we allow ourselves to be whirled away like the man who built his house upon the sand?

> *Therefore everyone who hears these words of Mine and acts on them, may be compared to a wise man who built his house on the rock. And the rain fell, and the floods came, and the winds blew and slammed against that house; and yet it did not fall, for it had been founded on the rock. Everyone who hears these words of Mine and does not act on them, will be like a foolish man who built his house on the sand. The rain fell, and the floods came, and the winds blew and slammed against that house; and it fell—and great was its fall. (Matthew 7:24-27[viii])*

Jesus tells this parable at the end of His Sermon on the Mount. Christ taught the disciples and those who gathered on the mountainside that day the Beatitudes and the Lord's prayer. Why end with this strange parable about where to build your house? He wants everyone, which includes us, to understand it is more than listening to His words. Applying those words to our lives is what makes the difference. When we hear the gospel, we can ignore the lessons and walk through life alone, or we can choose to believe in Christ, the Rock on which we stand.

Our most recent storm in life was on the farm. It was an evening of great loss when our combine caught fire. As I reflect on the evening, it was your typical storm. The rush of adrenalin as we did all we could do to put out the fire. The let-down moment when we realized our combine was a total loss, and I shed a tear. The anger because of the "Why me?" attitude. The justification that we did everything possible to prevent the fire. Fear of the unknown, as we awaited the outcome of the insurance claim. Do any of those emotions sound familiar? It doesn't matter what type of storm, your emotions will be up, down, and sideways, as you work through the situation. What makes the difference is how you work through your emotions with Christ.

A couple of hours after the fire, I told Jim I was angry at God because He allowed the fire to happen. After a short discussion and reflection, I realized I wasn't angry with God at all. I was angry about our loss and worried about the unknown. After a restless night's sleep, I was thankful no one was hurt and remembered we were blessed with crops to harvest.

Yes, there were blessings in the midst of the combine fire, God just needed to remind me. God became our Rock as we worked through the days after the fire. There were decisions, phone calls, and steps to walk through as we worked with the insurance company, and local equipment dealerships to locate a combine to complete our harvest.

As solutions fell into place, God revealed even more blessings. Farmers on the west coast of Florida recently lost their crops, their machinery, their barns and in some cases even their homes as a result of hurricane destruction. Who am I to question a combine fire when others have suffered a greater loss? Yes, Jim and I are truly blessed. Blessed we have the financial means to own a combine. Blessed to be farmers and help feed a hungry world. Blessed with friends, family and a church home. But most of all, we are blessed to stand upon the Rock, named Jesus Christ. A foundation which kept us strong during the storm.

Throughout this storm, we stand witness to Solomon's words. *"When the storms of life come, the wicked are whirled away, but the godly have a lasting foundation." (Proverbs 10:25).*

Yesterday we received one more blessing. A fair and just settlement from an amazing Christian insurance company. After the past few weeks, Jim and I can't imagine coping with the storms of life without the Rock by our side. Trials in life will come and go, but the Rock will always stand firm by your side, so chose to stand on the foundation of Christ today.

Picture taken only a few minutes after the fire began.

Catch Your Dirt

My granddaughter Reagan was on my lap and continually stretched her arm in the air as high as possible. She would open and close her hand repeatedly and I could not figure out why. After several times of this repetitive motion I asked, "What are you doing?"

"Catching your dirt Grandma."

The morning sunlight was shining brightly through the east windows and skylights. When she looked up, she could see dust floating in the air. She entertained herself as she attempted to catch Grandma's dirt. Of course, my first thought was, "Wow look at all the dust! Maybe I should clean more often."

After a time of reflection, I wondered why we as Christians don't raise our hands toward heaven more. When we raise our hands and pray, we can toss our dirt in the air to Jesus. We can allow it to float away as we make our requests known to Him.

The Old Testament is full of examples where the saints raised their hands toward heaven and prayed. Probably the most common example is Moses when God sent him to free the Israelites from slavery. With each plague God brought upon Egypt, Moses raised his hands and staff in the air as he prayed. God brought hardship upon the Egyptians as He tried to soften Pharaoh's heart so he would free the Israelites. Finally, after the loss of his son Pharaoh released the slaves. But his heart once again hardened, and the Israelites found themselves trapped against the sea. What did Moses do? He once again lifted his hands and staff toward heaven and prayed. One of the greatest miracles of all time happened as God parted the Red Sea and the Israelites walked across on dry land.

Remember when the Israelites battled the army of Amalek? As long as Moses held his hands in the air and lifted his staff toward heaven the Israelites would win the battle. But the moment he became exhausted and lowered his arms they would begin to lose. Aaron and Hur sat beside him and held up his arms until evening so God would give them the power to win the battle. (*Exodus 17*). What powerful examples of raising our hands toward heaven when we read about Moses!

While I walk in the mornings it is often a time of prayer. As I walked laps around the barn today, I had a heavy burden on my heart. I thought of Moses as I began to pray, so I raised my hands toward heaven. I have to admit, I gained a whole new respect for Moses too! Have you ever tried to pray with your hands in the air for very long? I felt like such a wimp! Regardless of my arm pain, I am convinced God saw this weak lady with her arms in the air as she prayed and had mercy on me. He probably looked down shook His head and said, "She's not Moses and she doesn't need me to part the Red Sea but I did see her toss a little dirt in the air." Then He reached down and caught my dirt.

Honestly the burden on my heart lifted. There will be more struggles and burdens one day but I will remember to raise my hands and pray to the Lord. Do you feel a heavy burden on your heart today? Raise your hands in prayer and toss your dirt to God. Then give Him the glory because He will catch your dirt too!

Play-Doh

"I want to play with Play-Doh®!" These are not words I long to hear from my grandchildren. Of all the toys, games, puzzles and books, Play-Doh is my least favorite playtime activity with the grandkids. It is messy, gooey, and slimy. It gets under your fingernails and stuck in the cookie cutters. Not to mention the mess it creates on the floor. But the main reason I don't like Play-Doh is I do all the work!

Make me a flower Grandma. Make me a cat. Make me a pig. Make me a snake. Make me a snowman. (Of course, he is brown because the colors have been mixed together.) Every sentence seems to start with "Make me a." Regardless of how much I dislike it I never say no, but seldom do I instigate the idea either. I understand it is actually good for them. It builds hand strength as they knead the dough. It opens up windows of creativity as they attempt to make creations on their own, before they turn the job over to me.

What an amazing similarity Play-Doh has to God as He shapes and molds our lives. Who we are in Christ, is a direct result of our reaction to God, the Potter. Especially when we pray, "Make me a better Christian, or make me more like You Lord." There are moments in our lives when we feel like the lump of clay.

> *The Lord gave another message to Jeremiah. He said, "Go down to the potter's shop, and I will speak to you there." So I did as he told me and found the potter working at his wheel. But the jar he was making did not turn out as he had hoped, so he crushed it into a lump of clay again and started over. (Jeremiah 18:1-4)*

We often look for scriptures like this when we face difficult circumstances. On the flip side, I believe God molds us through good events as well. As an example, I received positive feedback from a talk I gave on Sunday to a grief share group. God molds my heart and shapes me as I make decisions about future ministry. Is God calling me into some sort of grief ministry? Is He asking me to speak more? Do I continue to write and share my thoughts with my readers? All of these questions are wonderful exciting options. God continually molds and shapes me into the person He desires me to be.

When I tell God, "I am too old to start a ministry," He reminds me Sarah was way too old to bear a child but she did. When I tell God, "I'm not a great speaker," He reminds me Moses wasn't either. I made sure He remembered I am often like Peter. I'm all in until life becomes messy, gooey and slimy, and then I panic. God just smiled and said, "Yes, but go read Acts again and remember all Peter accomplished with the power of the Holy Spirit."

The bottom line is this. It doesn't matter how God shapes and molds you. Whether it is through good news or adversity it is still messy, gooey, and slimy as you work through the changes. Sometimes you just have to get out the broom and sweep away those items which are like globs of dough on the floor. Globs such as: I'm too old. I can't speak. I will let you down.

When we allow God to mold and shape us through the positive times in life it becomes much easier when He molds and shapes us through adversity. Life isn't always easy but as long as you keep your eye on the Prize, Jesus Christ, it will all be worth the messy, gooey, slimy changes along the way.

Childhood Confession

> *If we claim we have no sin, we are only fooling ourselves and not living in the truth. But if we confess our sins to him, he is faithful and just to forgive us our sins and to cleanse us from all wickedness. If we claim we have not sinned, we are calling God a liar and showing that his word has no place in our hearts. (1 John 1:8-10)*

One summer we decided to have one last fling of a vacation before our sons began life on their own. Matt would soon be a senior in college and Ryan's high school days were about to end as well. As is typical for our family we headed west toward the Dakotas, Montana and Wyoming. Matt had a summer job so he flew into South Dakota for a few days, but the rest of us drove.

It was a typical whirlwind vacation for the Rodman family. Short in days and high in mileage. Yet it was one of my most memorable family trips because they were so grown up. There were no disagreements from the back seat. Neither one asked, "Are we there yet?" I'm sure we sang *Tom Dooley* and the "Woohoo Song." (Our nickname for *Wolverton Mountain* because I sing the woohoo part.) We probably ate at hole-in-the-wall restaurants and loved the grease dripping from our chins as we added up the miles and reminisced. With every mile we traveled, we enjoyed grown-up conversations and walks down memory lane.

We were sharing one childhood memory after another when Matt looked at Ryan and said, "Do you remember when I used to unbuckle you in your car seat and then tell Mom and Jim you unbuckled yourself again?"

Jim and I both whipped our heads toward the back seat and simultaneously shouted, "It was you?"

When Ryan was little, we thought he was Houdini or a mechanical genius. Numerous times, Matt told us Ryan had unbuckled himself in his car seat. We would stop the car. Buckle him again and reprimand him. We did not understand how he could unbuckle at such a young age. Not in a million years did we ever think Matt was the culprit to simply get his brother in trouble! Fortunately, Ryan was too young to remember and I don't think the incidents scarred him for life.

I don't know why Matt brought up the story that day. Maybe he thought we knew it was him all those years ago or maybe deep down, confession is good for the soul. He pled guilty as charged and was slapped with a misdemeanor. I on the other hand felt as if I had committed a felony. I blamed Ryan for a crime he never committed and begged him for forgiveness that day.

We are all sinners and God longs to hear our confessions, even if it is a misdemeanor. We often feel as if we live a good, clean, decent life, so how could we possibly have sin to confess. The reality is that when we think we are sinless; it is a sin. Other times, our sin can be so heavy it weighs us down until we give it to the Lord. It doesn't matter how large or small your sin is, all sin is the same to Christ. We are fortunate Jesus Christ is in the forgiving business so don't tarry. Come before the Lord today and ask for forgiveness. Just as Matt discovered, you will soon realize confession is good for the soul.

Bluebirds and Mimosa Trees

It has been almost two years since Mom went home to be with the Lord. I definitely have days when I still miss her especially those moments when I want to share simple yet exciting news. News like, the bluebirds are home for the summer, or the mimosa tree is blooming.

Mom gave me the bluebird house so she was always the first person I called when the birds arrived home in the spring. She also gave me the mimosa tree which is seldom grown in central Ohio due to the cold winters. As I pulled in the drive, I noticed the tree was in full bloom for the first time in a couple of years. I was so excited I reached for my phone and then remembered I couldn't call her. I called Dad and shared my news with him instead. He was glad I called and said his tree was blooming too.

Dad is the best father ever but I truly desired a conversation with Mom. There was always excitement in her voice when we talked about bluebirds, flowers, and mimosa trees. I definitely miss those simple yet meaningful conversations.

I can't replace a conversation with Mom and neither can you and I replace a heart-to-heart talk with Jesus. Even if we call our closest friends, they will never comfort us like Jesus. God shares our joys, our happiness, as well as our pain and sorrow. He provides us with joy and amazement. He is the Protector of our hopes and dreams. Honestly, He even cares when my bluebirds return home and my mimosa tree blooms.

Christ longs to hear from us and be our "Mom" in times of loneliness. *Psalm 34* has beautiful verses about sharing life with the Lord. It starts with a little praise and moves into His unfailing love. It speaks of God's awesomeness which we often take for granted. We are reminded that He understands us and He provides us with protection. Then David wraps up the Psalm by reminding us that our hope is in Christ Jesus.

Let the godly sing for joy to the Lord;
it is fitting for the pure to praise him.

He loves whatever is just and good;
the unfailing love of the Lord fills the earth.

Let the whole world fear the Lord,
and let everyone stand in awe of him

He made their hearts,
so he understands everything they do.

But the Lord watches over those who fear him,
those who rely on his unfailing love.

We put our hope in the Lord.
He is our help and our shield.

Let your unfailing love surround us, Lord,
for our hope is in you.

(Psalm 34:1,5,8,15,18,20,22)

Spend some time with Jesus today. Share your simple and exciting joys with the Lord and allow yourself to be wowed by His awesomeness and His unfailing love. He will meet you where you are and give you hope for tomorrow.

Photo by: Christine Lynn Photography

Disgusting Tasks

Oh my, it has been one of those weeks. I have run in numerous directions and checked multiple items off of my to-do-list. One of those items was to purchase and drop off ibuprofen to Dad, which I did last night.

When I sat to visit with Dad for a few minutes, he held out his hand for me to trim his fingernails. Dad only has one hand, so he obviously can't trim them himself. I found the clippers and went to work. Then to my horror, off came his shoes and socks! I wanted to make a run for it, and escape to my car quickly! I immediately tried to avoid the task and said, "I will call the foot doctor Monday."

Well Dad hates to go to the foot doctor and claimed he would just do it himself. I had visions of him amputating a toe, or even toppling out of the chair onto his head as he began to lean forward. I obviously did not allow my ninety-one-year-old, one handed, father trim his own toe nails, so I took the clippers from him.

I completed the task at hand, and scrubbed my hands—several times. I visited a few minutes and headed for home. As I pulled out of his driveway, I gave my sister Janet a call to share my disgusting task story. It turns out she had her own disgusting task earlier in the day. She and her husband, Keith, had put a new toilet seat on Dad's toilet. We chuckled and tried to decide which one of us had the most repulsive job of the week. We talked about bleach, anti-bacteria soap, and peroxide as I tried to overcome my heebie-jeebies. While we talked, I worried about how contagious nail fungus might actually be, but our chuckles soon helped me forget. Janet shared our heebie-jeebies stories with her son last night. He rolled in laughter at our expense, especially the thought of trimming Dad's toe nails.

Sometimes we have to complete tasks we definitely do not enjoy in life, but we do them out of love. This was just one of those incidents. After all, he is my Dad and maybe he trimmed my toenails when I was little. (On second thought, I'm pretty sure Mom would have trimmed my nails.) Regardless, I faced the challenge at hand rather than running for home. (It definitely helped to know bleach, alcohol and peroxide were available upon the completion of my job.)

God gave Jonah a difficult task to accomplish one day as well. Jonah was instructed to go to Nineveh and warn the people that God's wrath would soon come upon them if they didn't repent of their wicked sins. But Jonah said, "Not me Lord! No way. I am not doing it."

He quickly made a run for it and hopped on the first boat he could find headed in the opposite direction of Nineveh. He didn't care about the people of Nineveh, and he had no desire to warn them about God's wrath.

Well it wasn't long until Jonah found himself in the belly of a great fish, where he began to pray. (He probably had the heebie-jeebies down there and asked God for some bleach.) Actually, he thanked God for saving his life. God had mercy for Jonah and had the fish spit him out on dry land. Jonah then went to Nineveh and warned the people that they were about to be destroyed. The people of Nineveh repented of their sins and God found mercy on them.

All of this would have been so much easier if Jonah had just accomplished the disgusting task the first time. All too often we act like Jonah and turn in the opposite direction from God. Our lives can sometimes be filled with one disgusting job after another and we question, "Where is our reward when we are obedient?" Our reward comes when we honor the Father (or in my case my Dad) and become His servant. Remember, one day you will stand before the Maker and He will say, *"Well done, my good and faithful servant...Let's celebrate together!" (Matthew 25:21).*

Suggested Scripture Reading
- Book of *Jonah*

Gnarly or Smiling

My husband, Jim, is worried because I seldom smile. He is afraid he has put this frown upon my face. I assured him he has done nothing wrong but at the same time I wonder why do I frown so much. God is worried about my lack of smile too. Every devotion, scripture, or self-improvement tip I received recently is about body language of which a smile is a huge part. I don't want to portray to others that I am unhappy because I am truly happy on the inside. I just don't show my joy on the outside.

    I love to laugh, have a good time and enjoy life. For example, last night we were at a Christian concert with friends. When I came out of the restroom stall someone came out of the stall right next to me, which I thought was my friend Pat. I continued my story I started before we entered. Suddenly I realized I was talking to a stranger. The sweet lady said, "If this is a funny story please continue."

    As Pat exited her bathroom stall I pointed and replied, "It's not funny, I just thought I was talking to her. Now my story about my husband's drive through the mountains is a hoot, but I don't think I have time to share that story before the concert starts."

    Instantly everyone in the restroom was smiling and laughing because I was jabbering to a stranger. Times like this make life fun, personable and enjoyable. It was a great start to a wonderful Spirit filled evening of music.

    Today I was parked beside the woods waiting for Jim to arrive on the tractor. I reflected on the restroom incident, verses to my lack of smile on a continual basis. My desire is to be the person who enjoys every moment in life rather than the person who appears to carry a heavy load. When I looked toward the woods my answer was in a tree. This particular tree was gnarly. The limbs went in every direction, twisted and curvy with no sense of pattern. Frazzled by life and the elements the tree leaned to the north yet its roots were still in the ground.

I thought to myself, "Yep—that's me! I feel exactly like this tree looks."

My life has become a bunch of gnarly branches with no direction, but praise the Lord my roots are still grounded in Christ! Since I published my first book the ministry sometimes overwhelms me. I constantly chase a problem, an opportunity, or just chase my own tail to keep up with life. (Can I just add my thoughts about Social Media and the time it consumes? On second thought, maybe it is a bad idea.) I love to learn new skills, but my learning curve is mind boggling right now. Even though I am excited about my life I have daily or weekly problems, confusion, decisions and frustrations which weigh me down. My branches are just a gnarly mess like the tree!

As I look over the big picture of this past year, I see how all of these moments, frustrations and sleepless nights are part of God's greater plan. He recently sent me an angel, John who is a publicist. John helps straighten my branches. I no longer worry about the right direction I seek his sound Christian advice instead. Even though our business relationship is new we both have deep roots in Christ with one common goal in mind—produce fruit for the kingdom of God.

I am reminded of *John 15:1-17* where Jesus refers of himself as the Vine and we are the branches. Sometimes God prunes our branches in ways we least expect, like our smile or our body language. I cannot produce good fruit for the kingdom of God without the godly leadership and guidance of others. Nor can I produce good fruit without the presence of Christ in my life. When I allow God to prune my branches of poor body language and the lack of a smile, I will draw closer to Him as we take this journey together. To God be the glory as He teaches me to produce more fruit for the kingdom of heaven!

> *When you produce much fruit, you are my true disciples. This brings great glory to my Father. (John 15:8)*

Suggested Scripture Reading
- *John 15:1-17*

Rules and Grace

Before you begin, please read the Parable of the Lost Son, found in *Luke 15:11-32*.

I was upset following a board meeting because the board wasn't obeying the rules for the ministry. I am all about the rules. Rules are there for a reason—to guide us, to protect us, and to keep us safe.

Following the rules isn't a trait I developed in my adult life either. My mother always said I never got in trouble as a child because I followed the rules. I can vividly remember a time I lied to my mom when I was about ten years old. It was the worst day of my childhood until I confessed to her later in the evening what I had done. In my mind rules have a purpose. It is cut and dry. All rules are to be followed. But on the flip side, none of us are perfect. I don't always follow the rules set by God. I can say I follow the Ten Commandments, but do I?

God blessed me with this personality, but it can also be a curse. I become more judgmental of others, especially when rules are broken. You could say I was a little peeved when no one on the board supported my comment that we did not intend to follow the rules. I felt like an outcast, like I had no right to point out the error of their ways.

If you are a rules person like me, you may have struggled with the story of the Prodigal Son. I used to relate to the other brother and his anger toward his father. Why in the world would you throw a party for him? I have been here with you this entire time. I have followed your rules. I have worked for you while he ran around and lived a wild life. I have done it exactly as you asked and he gets the party? Maybe there have been times in your life when you felt this way. Maybe you feel this way right now, because family situations can be difficult. Family can be your biological family, or like me, family can be the members of the board on which you serve.

But wait a minute—what about GRACE! Aren't we supposed to offer others grace like Christ offers it to us? This lesson was reinforced in my mind a few weeks after the board meeting. Yes, we didn't follow all the rules. Yes, it upset me because of my "rules" personality. But oh, how the power of the Holy Spirit showed up throughout the weekend event! You see, God doesn't care about our rules and regulations. He cares about our hearts and our souls. We can do it all wrong. We can act like the prodigal son and run astray. We can bend the rules for our own justification. But God will show up every time, put His hand of grace upon us and make everything right. His grace is a reason to celebrate! I want to attend His grace party, don't you!

Grace covers all of our sins, even the sin of being a strict rules follower. Rules help us live a good honest life, but grace covers our sins when we don't follow the guidelines. Grace wins every time! If you find yourself outside the party burdened by the rules of life, God covers you in grace too. As Christ's grace trickles down, for both the prodigal son and those who follow the rules, may we celebrate together because Grace is…

God's
Riches
At
Christ's
Expense

Old Friends

Today I received a book order from Idaho. It warms my heart to send the books to an old friend. Michele and I worked closely together many years ago. There were actually some days when I felt as if we worked a little too close and I'm sure she had days when she felt the same. We shared one big office with a partition between us. Private conversations, weren't always so private. Some days there was tension in the air, which neither of us wanted to address. As computer programmers, we were both great, but we also had our own styles. Often when we worked together on a project there would be a difference of opinion. We were actually both correct but occasionally a little stubborn and defensive because we wanted to do it our way.

During one of those tense times a good friend asked me if I prayed for Michele. I had to confess that I did not. I took her advice and began to pray for her and for our work relationship. Now I will be the first to admit some of those initial prayers came out slightly tainted with a little disdain. If you have a frustrating day in the office you will not pray, "Oh thank you Jesus for this wonderful office mate and the blessing she is to me." You start out with prayers more like, "Lord I know you love everyone but some days I just want my own office. I don't know why You put me in the same office with her. I need a solution now. AMEN!"

As time passed, my prayers turned to great compassion for Michele as I helped her walk through some difficult days. The more I prayed, the more her faith grew as she began to walk closer with the Lord. She was in a bad abusive marriage and ultimately was able to safely walk away from the relationship. I am so thankful God changed my heart and allowed me to be a prayer warrior for Michele throughout her darkest days. *"Are any of you suffering hardships? You should pray." (James 5:13a).*

A bad marriage wasn't the only bump in the road for Michele either. She was dismissed from two companies just prior to eligibility for pension and retirement benefits. On both occasions, she wasn't given a good reason for her dismissal. She persevered, forgave, and moved on with her life. If you look up the definition of forgiveness in the dictionary it might say, "See Michele." She is one of the most forgiving people I have ever met. Maybe when you overcome so many struggles in your life you learn to let go and trust God more. *"And forgive us our sins, as we have forgiven those who sin against us." (Matthew 6:12).*

I'm not sure if I will ever see my old friend in person again. Though I love to travel west it is a great distance between Ohio and Idaho. What I do know is we are both daughters of the King and one day we will walk the streets of gold together. But until then, we continue to stay in touch via social media. She posts the most beautiful pictures of the mountains, the snow, and all of her critters, both domestic and wild. She is truly living the life she always dreamed of—high in the mountains. I am glad God blessed her life with the mountain view of her dreams and a kind, loving, husband to share the experience. All those bumps in the road of life were worth it as she obtained her dream. *"Let us hold tightly without wavering to the hope we affirm, for God can be trusted to keep his promise." (Hebrews 10:23).*

God has taught me much through my old friend and those lessons can be summed up in three simple words. Prayer. Forgiveness. Hope. What wonderful gifts from God!

Overstuffed

I pulled up to the drive-through window at the bank today and riffled through a bunch of papers stuffed in my purse. I turned to the lady at the window, smiled and said, "It's in here somewhere. Just be patient with me please." It only took a couple more seconds, I spun back around with the check and deposit ticket in my hand. She smiled as I asked, "You never have this problem, do you?"

"Only when I need to clean my purse," she replied with a chuckle.

She sent my receipt back which I stuffed in my purse and off I drove to the post office. I mailed my package, received another receipt and stuffed it in my purse. I then stopped to get subs for our lunch. I was in such a flurry I put my billfold away before the clerk gave me the change. Since my purse was already full of papers and receipts, I stuffed the change in my pocket and left. Upon my return home, I stopped long enough to return all the papers, receipts and money to their appropriate places.

It had happened! My overstuffed life had overflowed into my purse and pockets. For the last month or two, my life has been a complete whirlwind. I stop every now and then, pull out the necessary item from my memory bank, and stuff the rest back down for later use. (No joke! My mind just jumped to tomorrow's board meeting. I stopped writing, sent a text message to the secretary requesting my topic be added the agenda. Now I can focus on writing again.) It is hard to focus on who and what is important, if you have too many items stuffed into your memory and schedule.

When your schedule is overloaded, who gets pushed aside first? Your spouse? Your children? God? It easily happens to all of us. We need to periodically reassess our priorities in life to stay on track. My husband and I had some "intense fellowship" last night which is a huge red flag of utter craziness in our home. Since we seldom fight, I know our overstuffed lives have trickled down, or verbally out, you could say. It is obviously time to assess our priorities again.

When we spin from one event to the next, it becomes especially hard to *"Be still in the presence of the Lord, and wait patiently for him to act." (Psalm 37:7).* If your life is overstuffed like mine, take time to reassess your priorities. In the last month, I have evaluated where my time is spent and who is in the path of the destruction because of my craziness. The board meeting which I referred to, this will be my last meeting. Even though it is a ministry very dear to my heart, I know God has called me in a different direction. So, it is time to step down and allow someone else to carry the ministry forward.

My number one priority is to carve out more time for God. Some days it may be prayer or Bible study. Other days, I may just sit and be still in His presence. Since I don't want to have "intense fellowship" daily or weekly, I will heed the advice given to us by the psalmist David. He prayed for peace. Peace for his family and friends in Jerusalem. I too will pray for peace for my family and friends.

Pray for peace in Jerusalem.
May all who love this city prosper.
O Jerusalem, may there be peace within your walls
and prosperity in your palaces.
For the sake of my family and friends, I will say,
"May you have peace."
For the sake of the house of the Lord our God,
I will seek what is best for you, O Jerusalem.
(Psalm 122:6-9)

Dare to Dream

A friend of mine posted this quote on Facebook. *"What you dare to dream of, dare to do."* It was written beside the 1930 nursing school graduation picture of her Grandma, Sara Jane Shoaf. I read the quote several times and allowed myself to ponder those words. *"What you dare to dream of, dare to do."*

Dare—have the courage to do something. Dream—a cherished aspiration, or ambition. If you and I aspire to accomplish goals in our lives, we need to include God in our plans. His plans are always greater than our plans. He is the one who gives us the courage to succeed in life.

The first Bible verse which comes to mind to support this quote is, *"For I can do everything through Christ, who gives me strength." (Philippians 4:13)*. But I wanted a biblical character or a biblical story which proved *Philippians 4:13*.

My research led me to Caleb. He is first introduced to us in the Old Testament in the book of Numbers. Caleb was one of the twelve spies which Moses sent into the land of Canaan to investigate the territory. Upon their return, ten of the spies shook in their boots. They found walled cities and giants who lived in the land and they wanted no part of a battle against them. But not Joshua and Caleb. They were ready to go to battle. Caleb even said, *"Let's go at once to take the land. We can certainly conquer it!" (Number 13:30)*.

Caleb was faithful to God and he stood upon the promises of the Lord. The city walls, the giants, and the people who lived there were small compared to the strength which his God would provide. Because of his faithfulness, God told Moses to give Caleb and his tribe the hill country in Canaan which he had just walked upon as his inheritance.

Fast forward forty-five years and we pick up the story of Caleb in the book of Joshua. The Israelites have wandered in the dessert for years and years. All of the naysayers who refused to go to battle are now deceased. The battles have begun for the Promised Land and Caleb reminds Joshua the Lord has already granted him the beautiful hill country.

> *Today I am eighty-five years old. I am as strong now as I was when Moses sent me on that journey, and I can still travel and fight as well as I could then. So give me the hill country that the Lord promised me. You will remember that as scouts we found the descendants of Anak living there in great, walled towns.* **But** *if the Lord is with me, I will drive them out of the land, just as the Lord said. (Joshua 14:10b-12 - Emphasis added)*

Eighty-five and ready for battle! I hope I am that feisty when I reach my eighties. A great pastor once told me anytime you see a "but" in scripture you want to pay attention to what comes next. *"**But** if the Lord is with me."* What an important statement in this scripture!

I am inspired by Caleb's story of perseverance. He was there. He was ready to conquer the walled cities and the giants who lived there. He was disappointed by his peers. He was sent to wander in the desert for forty-five years, and not by his choice. He dreamed of this beautiful land for years and years but he never gave up hope.

Upon his return, I can almost hear Caleb say, *"What you dare to dream of, dare to do. I have dreamed of this land for forty-five years.* ***But*** *if the Lord is with me, I will conquer this land today and I receive the blessing which God has given me."*

Obstacles in our lives often cause us to give up, shake in our boots, or throw in the towel. Don't let life steal your hopes and dreams. Dreaming worked for Caleb. Dreaming worked for Sara Jane Shoaf. And dreaming will work for you when you seek the strength and support of the Lord.

The Fall and The Rise

I still remember the phone call I received from my sister while on vacation several years ago. She called to inform me that our nephew Heath had embezzled money from the family farm to support his addiction to prescription narcotics. Though many of us were suspicious or even knew there was a problem, we ignored the signs. We did not realize how horrible his addiction had become. Now several years later, if you ask Heath about this day, he will describe it as the best and worst day of his life.

The fall—The moment Heath's world crashed down as the truth was revealed. Since Adam and Eve ate of the forbidden fruit there has been sin in the world. You and I are no exception. Though it seemed Heath's sin was huge at the time, we all fall short of the glory of God.

As the day unfolded Heath was given two options. He could leave the family farm and admit himself to rehab, or he could face criminal charges. With the unbelievable grace shown to him, he wept a sigh of relief. His drug addiction and embezzlement were finally out in the open and he knew he needed help. The opportunity for rehab was now right in front of him.

The rise—The moment grace appeared for his addiction problem and the theft which had occurred. He wanted and he needed help. He chose rehab, or in this case, the grace extended by his family. Before Heath left for rehab, he prayed the most heartfelt, tearful prayer he had ever prayed. He gave his life to Christ on the back deck of his home as he asked forgiveness of his many sins.

Grace appeared for this lost world the moment Christ gave up His life on the cross, defeated Satan, and rose again.

The faith—Confession of sins followed by blind faith. Heath had no idea what was in store for him at the rehab center. No idea of the pain he would experience from withdrawals, or the emotional rollercoaster which was ahead. Yet he walked by faith through those doors and admitted himself to rehab, knowing Christ was with him on his journey. *"Faith shows the reality of what we hope for; it is the evidence of things we cannot see." (Hebrews 11:1).*

We rallied around him with prayers as he walked through the necessary steps of recovery. We knew drug addiction was difficult to overcome, but not impossible. Everyone reacts differently in family situations such as these, so emotions raged in our family for many months. Yet I am a firm believer that time heals, or at least mellows the heart when you allow love to enter.

The hope—There is hope in all situations, and Heath found his hope at the foot of the cross. Though rehab was a necessary part of his recovery, his hope was in Jesus Christ. Christ reached down, and took his hand the day he gave his life to the Lord. Jesus Christ lifted him out of the pit, and set his feet on solid ground. I have seen a strong faith emerge in Heath as he walks with Christ daily and knows his source of strength comes from the Heavenly Father above.

The love—The moment Heath's faithful wife, Trisha, realized she could love Heath unconditionally, because God loves her unconditionally. She stood by him through this difficult time in their lives. Sometimes going through the motions, and sometimes with a glimpse of the man she married. Her faithfulness to their wedding vows paid off as love emerged and triumphed once again.

Now six years later, Heath and Trisha's journey has taken them to a new life, in a new state, and a new business. They now have a new battle as Trisha suffers from bi-polar II issues. Trisha and Heath recently knelt on the carpet in their home in Kentucky, and she prayed a heartfelt tearful prayer similar to the words Heath prayed many years ago. She asked for forgiveness, for healing, and for God's will to be done. God wrapped them in His arms of comfort and gave them peace.

Christ gives all of us faith, hope and love. Through the ups and downs of rehab, and counseling through mental health issues, drug addiction, marital struggles, arguments and disagreements love has always prevailed. Heath continues to stand by Trisha's side, just as she did for him a few years before. Though this journey has been one of great difficulty, their example of unconditional love gives them a testimony to share with a lost world. A world which struggles with addiction and mental health issues. Their openness to share their faith story is because Christ is love, and without Christ there would be no hope for a hurting world.

> *Three things will last forever—faith, hope, and love—and the greatest of these is love.*
> *(1 Corinthians 13:13)*

Points to Ponder
- The Fall—What situation in your life caused you to fall away from Christ?
- The Rise—Did you come to Christ at that moment and ask for forgiveness? If not, why not today?
- The Faith—Even faith as small as a mustard seed can change your life. (*Matthew 17:20)*. What small seed of faith do you have to overcome the difficulties in your life?
- The Hope—How can you allow God to be your source of hope for each moment?
- The Love—We all express love differently, but Christ's love for us never changes. Recall a moment in your life when you knew God's love was real and steadfast. Focus on Christ's love as you overcome the fall.

Break the Silence

When the weather isn't favorable to walk outside, I walk laps in our shop. I listen to Christian music while I walk but I cannot hear the music throughout the building unless I carry my phone. Before I began my morning walk, my son Matt installed an app on my phone which allowed me to use his speaker system for the shop and offices. He gave me an abbreviated lesson on the controls and I began to walk.

A couple of weeks later I started my app and began to walk. I couldn't hear any music through the speaker in the shop and my abbreviated lesson didn't cover this problem. I turned the music on and off. Nothing. I cranked the volume as loud as it would go. Nothing. I turned the volume up and down. Nothing. I was totally perplexed and frustrated.

The last time Matt used the speaker system he turned off the shop speaker. Plus, I didn't know Matt was working in his office. He checked his phone and computer trying to figure out why the music suddenly came on and off. When I cranked the volume all the way up, he was startled and he wondered what in the world was going on. Why was the music suddenly loud and sporadic?

Then he remembered the app was on my phone. He emerged from his office and exclaimed, "You're here that explains the problem. I wondered why the music went crazy!"

I smiled and responded, "I'm sorry. I'm can't hear music out here. Can you hear it in your office?"

We had a good laugh as he gave me another lesson on the app and showed me how to turn the different speakers on and off.

When the music blared, Matt was more than just a little startled. The unexpected volume made him cover his ears and scramble for the volume control on his phone. In the same manner, Elihu describes the loud voice of God. *"My heart pounds as I think of this. It trembles within me. Listen carefully to the thunder of God's voice as it rolls from his mouth. God's voice is glorious in the thunder. We can't even imagine the greatness of his power."* (Job 37:1, 2, 5).

Elihu urges Job to look at everything God created and His daily miracles which is a sign of God's omnipresence. He reminds Job that if God can control all of creation He surely knows of your pain and suffering. Even though God was silent throughout Job's test of faith He still cared deeply for him. Elihu pleaded with Job to understand that his faith in God was more important than understanding why God was silent at this moment in his life. Ironically Elihu's speech brought an end to God's silence. God began to question Job explaining that He was and still is an omnipotent God.

Just as my speaker in the shop was silent, God is often silent with us. We may never understand our pain and suffering yet we need to remain faithful and trust Him. God shows Job that silence doesn't mean He has forgotten him, it was to strengthen him. Just like Job we may not comprehend God's silence, but He has a plan to stretch and grow our faith. God simply wants us to remain faithful throughout the journey.

Elihu's description of God's voice reminds us to listen to God when He boldly speaks. Often times we try to speak for God rather than listen to the Holy Spirit. We need to heed the promises of *Psalm 37:7a "Be still in the presence of the Lord, and wait patiently for him to act."* God speaks in many different ways as He did with Job. Through the Word, the Holy Spirit, our circumstance, and even our friends when the timing is right.

Suggested Scripture Reading
- *Job 37–42*

The Donkey

Several months ago, there was a donkey in my life. I knew the problem existed, yet I didn't know how to move past the problem. The donkey was conflict at my part-time job for the church. Eventually I realized it was best for me to resign and gracefully walk away. It was definitely the best decision for me, and I believe it was best for the church also. Unrest in the church is not God's desire for the body of Christ. But the donkey, or should I say the underlying tension was still there.

Sunday was Pastor Matt's last Sunday at the church. Jim urged me to return and say goodbye for closure. It was a difficult decision with the donkey in the room, but we went. I heard a wonderful sermon, by a great pastor, who ironically was part of the conflict and the donkey. In his sermon, Matt said we need to look past the donkey and see what is on the other side. He was referring to the story of Balaam and the donkey, which is found in *Numbers 22-24*. If you aren't familiar with the story, or need a refresher, let me bring you up to speed.

In hopes that God would turn against the Israelites, the Moabites hired the sorcerer Balaam to speak a curse over Israel. God told Balaam not to go to Moab, but Balaam's love for money as a sorcerer was so great, he ignored God's warning.

As Balaam traveled toward Moab, an angel of the Lord blocked the roadway three times so the donkey could not pass. This upset Balaam and he beat the donkey each time. After the third time, God gave the donkey the ability to speak. (Yes, a real-life Mr. Ed, the talking horse, in biblical days.) Once the donkey had Balaam's attention, God opened Balaam's eyes so he could see the angel. He instantly realized he should not have beaten the donkey and that he was wrong for going to Moab to curse the Israelites.

He told the angel he would return home, but the angel told him to continue toward Moab. Once he arrived, he was to speak only the words the Lord gave him. So, Balaam did as the angel requested. Each time Balak asked Balaam to speak, Balaam prayed to the Lord first and the Lord had him speak blessings over the Israelites. Balak, the king of Moab, had no idea how difficult it would be to battle God.

Pastor Matt taught us to look past the donkey to see what is on the other side. When Balaam beat the donkey, he didn't see the angel of the Lord on the other side. The donkey in the church office was personality conflicts. I was so frustrated and angry at times I couldn't see what was beyond the donkey.

Jim is known for his saying, "There's not much education in the second kick of a mule." I wish I had followed his advice, or even Balaam's example of three times. It was way beyond the second or third kick before my eyes were opened and I understood my ministry in the church office was complete. For unknown reasons, I waited until the mule had kicked me to the point of agony before I looked to the other side and resigned. God calls us to serve, but He also calls us to stop, turn, and take a different road when our ministry is complete.

What I found on the other side of the donkey was an angel in the form of my book, *Bloom Where You're Planted*. The ministry continues to bloom from my book and God uses me in ways I never imagined. For Pastor Matt, a pastoral position in his home town was beyond the donkey. He was a great asset to the Richwood Church of Christ and the Richwood community. He will be greatly missed by many. At his new church, he will continue to do what he does best, preach and teach the gospel. But this time it will be back in his hometown to raise his family.

I'm glad Jim encouraged me to return and hear Pastor Matt's final sermon before their move. We had the opportunity to hug one another and see past the donkey. When we are obedient to God's Word and forgive one another, our ministry will prosper.

> *If another believer sins, rebuke that person; then if there is repentance, forgive. Even if that person wrongs you seven times a day and each time turns again and asks forgiveness, you must forgive. (Luke 17:3-4)*

Suggested Scripture Reading
- *Numbers 22-24*

My ministry continues to grow as a result of my *Bloom Daily Devotional Series Book 1, Bloom Where You're Planted.* A result of this growth is the Bible study I wrote about Mary Magdalene. Mary was a woman who was transformed from evil spirits into a resilient servant of Christ. Download this free Bible study, **Mary Magdalene—A Woman of Resilience** at www.MaryRodman.com/BookBonuses.

The Storm

The winds swirl and come from the north.
Ice and snow quickly cover the earth.

The storm outside begins to rage.
The ground below becomes the stage.

Ice and snow gather so quick.
As it leaves a coat upon every stick.

Storms in our lives are just the same.
Anger swirls as we point and blame.

Conflict and troubles are Satan's game.
Keeps us from sharing God's great name.

The Maker of storms can calm the seas.
But He also cares for you and me.

The Holy Spirit enters when you pray.
"Heavenly Father be near me today.

Walk by my side forever more.
I'm filled with your presence to the core.

Walking with You throughout each storm.
I feel your Comfort, oh so warm.

Gather me close to Your side once again.
Wrapped in your arms of love. Amen."

Zip-Line

I posted a picture on Facebook of my granddaughter Reagan gliding down the zip-line at her gymnastics class. The caption said, "Reagan loves the zip-line. We should all have this much fun every day. We would be better Christians if we did!"

When Nana saw my post she said, "I love her little weeeeee and ahhhhhhh!"

Grammy said, "I love that smile!"

And I added, "Watch her eyes. Cracks me up!"

In all of her excitement her little eyes zipped back and forth as she checked for her landing and watched where she had been. There was pure joy in her five second ride. The children look forward to their trips down the zip-line at the end gymnastics class. The goal is to help them build arm muscles but to the little ones it is the thrill of the ride.

God wants us to experience that same pure joy on a daily basis. A moment in the day when nothing else matters except our love relationship with Christ. Yesterday my moment was the beautiful snow scenery. The frost and snow hung in the trees as it glistened in the morning sun. Only God can paint a picture so beautiful. Often it is the quiet time with God as I pray. I love when His Word touches my heart or when the Holy Spirit nudges me to pay close attention. Oh, what joy throughout these moments in my life.

This week, *Matthew 9:13* spoke to me. Jesus said, *"Now go and learn the meaning of this Scripture: 'I want you to show mercy, not offer sacrifices.' For I have come to call not those who think they are righteous, but those who know they are sinners."* The Pharisees ridiculed Jesus for eating with disreputable sinners and Christ reprimanded them for their narrowminded self-righteous thoughts. The words, *"I want you to show mercy, not offer sacrifices,"* resonates in my mind. He pointed His finger at the Pharisees because they had it all wrong, but He also points His finger at you and me. Are we any different today? What is more important, our social image or our love for Jesus Christ?

In *Matthew 9:13* Jesus is referring to this Old Testament verse. *"I want you to show love, not offer sacrifices. I want you to know me more than I want burnt offerings." (Hosea 6:6).* The love or mercy God is referring to is a love relationship with Him. He doesn't ask for our good deeds, righteous attitudes, or fake lives. He wants all of us, every part of our hearts and souls to be in a love relationship with Him. Don't attend church, take communion, serve others, read the Bible, and pray as a ritual. Do them because you love God and desire a stronger relationship with Him.

Reagan's eyes zipped back and forth as she watched for her landing. But our eyes need to stay focused on Christ. God's desire is for us to grow closer to Him each day. When we do this. When we get it right, when we understand that our love relationship with the Lord is the key to contentment. Then we will experience pure joy in our daily lives. Psalms and Proverbs are filled with references about joy but pure joy always points us back to a love relationship with the King of Kings.

Like Reagan on her zip-line, life can speed by you in a five second thrilling ride or you can treasure those moments of pure joy with the Lord. Let your heart be filled with love as you spend time with Jesus. He has called you into a love relationship with Him. He is there in the beauty of the snow. He is there as you watch a child ride a zip-line. He is there when you read scriptures and as you observe communion. He is listening when you pray. He is everywhere. Open your heart to Christ's great love as you begin to know Him more. Then you will find pure joy in your daily life.

Suggested Scripture Reading
- *Matthew 9:9-13*
- *Hosea 6:4-7*
- Look for references of joy in *Psalms* and *Proverbs*

Happy Anniversary

I have written many devotions about my husband, Jim. My all-time favorite is "Bobsled Ride," which is about the time he drove like Dale Earnhardt, Jr. in the mountains. We have wonderful memories of our travels around the United States as we enjoy God's creations. In addition to our stories of faith, friendship, farm life, and family, he provides me with great humorous material.

Tomorrow we will celebrate our twenty-seventh wedding anniversary. As I look back through the years, I cherish all of our wonderful times and memories together. Like all marriages not every moment has been rosy. We have had our ups and downs, our battles and occasionally those unkind words.

For example, yesterday I shared exciting news about this book. You could say I was walking on the clouds. He was frustrated over some farm paperwork and his frame of mind was not positive about life as a whole. He pointed out the negative side of my opportunity and popped my bubble. As a result, I snapped back and stomped out the door to meet a friend for lunch.

But here is where love, forgiveness and friendship take hold. Where the rubber meets the road and I had a decision to make. I could stay mad at him the rest of the day or I could forgive him. I will always choose forgiveness because he is the one I share my life with. Two miles down the road I called him. I had only shared half of my good news and I couldn't wait to tell him the rest of the story. Why? He is my best friend through the good, the bad, and the ugly. Even in those bubble popping moments I love him with all my heart.

The day before this incident I read *Proverbs 17:9* as part of my morning Bible study. It seemed to jump off the page at me because it truly describes our marriage. I don't believe it was a coincidence either. I felt God's nudge to focus on the words. God knew the next day I would need to remember Solomon's words of advice about forgiveness when we had our small tiff.

"Love prospers when a fault is forgiven, but dwelling on it separates close friends." (Proverbs 17:9). Jim and I are close friends, totally in love and we share life together. We both have our faults but love continues to prosper. The reason we have a good marriage is forgiveness. It didn't take me five minutes to forgive him for his bubble popping attitude. In the same manner, he forgives me when the tables are turned. A Christ centered marriage has to include forgiveness because Christ forgives us.

My favorite memory of Jim is the day we met. I knew from the first moment he was someone special. He was a perfect gentleman, easy to talk to and we had so much fun together. His smile and words were just as encouraging as they are today. He was a gift from God and an answer to my prayers. It was because of Jim's faith, his prayers, and his love for the Lord that I rededicated my life to Christ early in our marriage.

This current journey of writing devotions and speaking of God's love would not be possible without the love and support of my wonderful husband. (He loves the word wonderful which I used to describe him in my first book.) But I chose wonderful because it is true. I love the husband he is, the provider he has been and continues to be for our family and our farm. The love he shows me, our children, our grandchildren and his love for the Lord never cease. He never hesitates to help a friend in need or even a stranger. God made him extra special with a huge heart full of love. Yes, my husband is wonderfully made by God.

Jim loves the phrase, "marriage is falling in and out of love over and over again with the same person." I believe this is true but I also believe every time I fall back in love with him, it is a deeper richer love. A love this strong is only possible because of the God's grace. A grace which trickles down from above and into the crevasses of our lives and who we are as a couple.

So, here's to you. Happy Anniversary to my wonderful husband, Jim Rodman! Just as my car license plate says, I LOVE JR. I love you with all of my heart. May we always allow love to prosper and our faults to be forgiven as we fall in and out of love over and over again for many years to come!

Sandcastles

While we relaxed on the beach in Mexico, my friend Angie and I watched a man build a sandcastle. He used all the necessary tools to pack the sand and made numerous trips to the shore for water. Throughout the process, he was methodical and precise on where he positioned the next bucket of sand. Slowly a castle began to form, then five pillars in front of the castle. Each of those pillars contained a letter, B-E-C-K-S. Beck's is the company which sponsored our trip to the resort. What a wonderful way to thank them and share his beautiful work of art with everyone.

We introduced ourselves to he and his wife and visited with them. He shared that it gives him the opportunity to use his artistic talent. He is obviously passionate about sandcastles and he definitely has a creative gift. He spent five or six hours building the castle. A creation for our enjoyment, even though it was a temporary work of art on the shore of Mexico.

When we walked the beach the next afternoon, we found it was slowly being destroyed. Maybe a little by the waves, but mostly by people who dug into the castle and walked across it. Since we knew the amount of time he spent, it broke our hearts to see it destroyed so quickly.

To our astonishment, when we walked the beach the next afternoon, Anthony had built another sandcastle. This one was larger and more detailed than the first. He had written Mexico 2018 and used the Beck's logo. It was our last afternoon on the beach, so we have no idea how long this beautiful castle lasted.

It was such a selfless act on Anthony's part. He thanked the sponsor of the trip and created a work of art for everyone's enjoyment. Not once, but twice. He did not seek any glory or recognition. He simply loves to build sandcastles. He gladly shares his story with anyone who stops to admire his art work. He spent countless hours building the sandcastles, knowing they would soon be washed away by the waves and destroyed. What an unselfish gift, to share his talent and time with others!

Christ too lived a life full of unselfishness. But his life was spotless and free of sin. Many challenged Him. Despised Him. Falsely accused Him. Yet He never loved his accusers any less than he loves you and me. *The Message* describes Christ's unselfishness with these words.

> *This is the kind of life you've been invited into, the kind of life Christ lived. He suffered everything that came his way so you would know that it could be done, and also know how to do it, step-by-step. He never did one thing wrong, not once said anything amiss. They called him every name in the book and he said nothing back. He suffered in silence, content to let God set things right. He used his servant body to carry our sins to the Cross so we could be rid of sin, free to live the right way. His wounds became your healing. You were lost sheep with no idea who you were or where you were going. Now you're named and kept for good by the Shepherd of your souls. (1 Peter 2:21-25 MSG)*

One selfless man, built sandcastles on the beach. One by one, he continues to build them for others to enjoy. When he does, he knows they are temporary works of art on the shores wherever he vacations. I wonder, how many sandcastles will he build in his lifetime? How many lives will he touch with his artistic ability? Those answers I will never know.

One selfless Savior gave us an example of how to love unconditionally. His love for the world was so deep, He even carried our sins to the cross. He died and rose again, so we might live eternally with Him. His love is not temporary, it is forever.

Will you follow Christ's example of unselfishness and reach out to someone who needs Jesus Christ today? In your lifetime, how many lives will you change as you share the gospel of Christ? That answer you will never know this side of heaven!

Sandcastle by Anthony Downing in Mexico.

Follow Christ More

A five-day trip to Mexico with my BFF sounded like a great time, and it was! We relaxed, enjoyed great conversations, and even some philosophical discussions about how God constantly works in our lives. We swam with the dolphins, which was an absolute blast. (If you ever have the opportunity, I highly recommend you do a foot push by a dolphin.) We ate some wonderful food and took in a little too much sun. But at the same time, on our last day there I began to get homesick for my loved ones back home. Especially my husband and my granddaughter Reagan, who I babysit two days a week. But this vacation made me realize what I missed the most in my life was a better relationship with God.

Even though I speak about God's love and I write devotions, sometimes I feel somewhat empty inside. I want God to use me in powerful ways, and I constantly search for His will in my life. What God wants is for me to quit searching and just follow Him wholeheartedly. I'm prone to details, plans, and schedules. For this need-to-know-the-details gal, it has become a huge barrier in my spiritual journey. How do I let go, when I don't know the who, what, where, when and why of the next step in my life?

This is where God's omnipotent power showed me, I can let go of the details and learn to follow. Before I left home, I quickly searched the bookshelf for a couple of books to take along. I removed three books from the shelf which I had not read. I quickly looked at the authors, and eliminated one.

I arrived in Mexico with the two books. One was a devotional which would not fill a lot of beach time, so I tossed it back in the suitcase. The second was *Chasing God* by Angie Smith. By chapter two, I knew it was no coincidence that I was supposed to read this book. She described herself as a need-to-know-the-details type of gal. God had plans to open my eyes to a life where the details aren't always for me to worry about. Angie's fun-loving style of writing immediately drew me in to her words of wisdom.

I saw myself in her story. The person who pays so much attention to details I find it difficult to simply allow myself to trust God in the journey. In the midst of her words, I realized I too chase God. What I desire is to stop the chase and follow wherever He leads. I felt a tug at my heart and a burden lift from my soul as I bowed my head in prayer. It was a prayer of total submission and a promise to follow wherever this life journey leads.

I can't say I have a key Bible verse or one Bible story to drive this point home, but the scriptures are full of examples of those who simply walked by faith which is exactly what God calls you and I to do. He wants us to walk with Him so closely we feel the nudge of the Holy Spirit, rather than worry about the details of the journey ahead.

One example, the woman who touched the hem of Jesus' garment. She didn't know if she would be healed or if she would be ridiculed as she walked among the crowd as an unclean woman. But she trusted enough to reach out to Christ.

The woman caught in adultery certainly didn't expect forgiveness the day her sins were exposed either. She was about to be stoned to death! She had no clue that the moment she met Jesus her life would be changed forever.

And what about Peter? He couldn't decide if he was a need-to-know-the-details guy or one who could walk by faith and follow Christ. One minute he walked on water and the next he denied Christ three times because he was afraid of what might happen.

All I know is Christ wants me to chase Him less and follow Him more. Each day is a journey and where He leads, I do not know. The one important step I know is when I wake each day and listen to the Holy Spirit, it will be a good day because I am following Christ instead of chasing Him.

My foot push by the dolphins.

The Fire

My nephew Joe and his family lost all they own in a house fire last week. Joe happened to go home about noon and found smoke bellowing from their home. While he waited for the fire department to arrive, he was only able to save their beloved dog, Judy. Seven fire departments were there to assist but they could not save their home.

At one point a fireman asked if he could salvage anything from their kitchen. Joe asked for their new pans which hung on the wall. The fireman returned and said, "I'm sorry you no longer have kitchen wall." So not even a pan was retrieved. Later in the day and upon the firemen's request my brother bulldozed the final walls of their home inward as they watched the remaining structure burn to the ground.

Joe and Laura were told the fire most likely began to smolder while they were asleep the night before. They were not only shocked to hear those words but in a state of shock from all which had happened. In spite of their loss, they were extremely thankful no one was hurt.

Over the next few days they received an outpouring of love. Family, friends, acquaintances and people they barely knew asked what they needed or how they could help. All too often we help during these circumstances but turn a blind eye to others in need. By no means am I saying Joe and Laura didn't deserve the gifts they received, but what about those who already have very little. Sometimes we are so blessed we forget to give out of love.

The story of the poor widow which can be found in *Luke 21:1-4* is a biblical example of giving from the heart. Many rich people dropped their gifts in the collection box but the widow gave all she had which was two small coins. That was it! She wanted no recognition. She didn't get a tax write-off for her donation. She never asked for financial handouts either. It was simply a gift of love. Love she had for God.

The state of your heart is the difference between giving and giving out of love. The rich people gave but the widow gave out of love. We all give at one time or another. The offering plate comes down the aisle and we give. When the envelope is passed around the office, we give. When our favorite charities solicit, we give. It is Christmas time so we give. But if these gifts aren't given with love, they mean nothing.

1 Corinthians 13 is known as the love chapter and the last verse is one of the most quoted Bible verses of all times. *"And now these three remain: faith, hope and love. But the greatest of these is love." (1 Corinthians 13:13 NIV).* But the beginning of the chapter explains why love is so important. It is the foundation of our Christian faith. It is the reason we should give endlessly and seek no glory. Just like the poor widow who gave all she had we should give out of love.

> *If I could speak all the languages of earth and of angels, but didn't love others, I would only be a noisy gong or a clanging cymbal. If I had the gift of prophecy, and if I understood all of God's secret plans and possessed all knowledge, and if I had such faith that I could move mountains, but didn't love others, I would be nothing. If I gave everything I have to the poor and even sacrificed my body, I could boast about it; but if I didn't love others, I would have gained nothing. (1 Corinthians 13:1-3)*

Christ never asks us to give to others but He commands us to love one another. Giving is simply a result of loving. All Joe and Laura received was the result of an outpouring of love because those giving had nothing to gain but love itself.

When we leave this world, our possessions will remain on this earth. Our spiritual gifts will no longer be needed as they are earthly gifts. But love will remain. So, in all you do, *"Let love be your highest goal!" (Corinthians 14:1a)*. The next time you give, don't give because you have to, give because you love!

Sorry Grandma

This year my granddaughters Mya and Reagan helped decorate the Christmas tree. Considering their ages, five and two-and-a-half respectively, you can imagine what the tree looked like. Most of the ornaments were between five foot which was step stool height for Mya, and three foot which was Reagan's prime target area. They were grouped in clusters which covered about two thirds of the tree. I was able to get a few decorations up high and persuade them to adorn the other side of the tree occasionally. Unfortunately, not all of my ornaments are child proof. We had a few casualties along the way which was usually followed by, "Sorry Grandma," as I went for the broom and dustpan.

When my sons were little, I'm sure I grumbled for them to spread the decorations evenly around the tree or to be careful with breakable ornaments. But now it is all about memories with the grandkids. I don't care which decorations they use or where they hang. It doesn't matter how many glass bulbs they break because I have too many decorations anyway. What I do remember is their sweet little voices saying, "Sorry Grandma."

I don't know if time changed me or whether I am more patient with my grandkids. Maybe I have mellowed because of my Christian walk. Regardless, I am thankful for the change and enjoy the moment rather than stressing about the details of the tree. Hmm…it sounds a little like the difference between Martha and Mary found in the gospel of Luke.

I believe we need both Martha and Mary in this world. If there were no Martha's how would work and growth ever be accomplished? God gave me spiritual gifts such as the gift of administration (I claim this one heavily), faith, encouragement, and more.

All spiritual gifts come with pitfalls and my gift of administration is no exception. I can become so focused on the task I forget the purpose is to glorify Jesus Christ. I have to be extremely cautious not to be overbearing and rigid in my ways. Sometimes I desire so much control I leave no place for God. Unfortunately, when I become task-oriented Martha pops out in me every time and takes charge. But when Martha emerges is when I most need Mary to show up and remind me it is about Jesus! I have to remember it is more important to seek God's will than to put my personal agenda into action.

Sometimes my Martha personality is the thorn in my side which Paul mentions. I need to submit to Christ and show my weakness which is my desire to be in control of the situation and all the details. When I finally submit, I focus on Christ and follow His lead.

> *I was given a thorn in my flesh, a messenger from Satan to torment me and keep me from becoming proud. Three different times I begged the Lord to take it away. Each time he said, 'My grace is all you need. My power works best in weakness.' So now I am glad to boast about my weaknesses, so that the power of Christ can work through me. That's why I take pleasure in my weaknesses, and in the insults, hardships, persecutions, and troubles that I suffer for Christ. For when I am weak, then I am strong. (2 Corinthians 12:7b-10)*

We all have spiritual gifts which can become our weaknesses. I have witnessed many with the gift of shepherding who shepherd so much they neglect their own families. They feel it is their duty to care for the entire world but forget those they love the most.

Regardless of your gift or the weakness it causes, remember when you are weak, Christ will give you strength. Follow the example set by Mary and sit at the feet of Jesus. Let Him know you have fallen into the pitfalls of your spiritual gifts. If you don't know how to pray maybe you could start with, "Sorry God. I wasn't careful and there were a few casualties along the way."

Suggested Scripture Reading
- *Luke 10:38-42*

The Key

Lately the unlock button on my key fob doesn't always work. Yet I never take the time to get a new battery. I figure as long as the SUV unlocks, why bother. But after today, it is a higher priority to replace the battery.

As I left the grocery store, I pushed my cart through several inches of snow. Just as I neared the back of the SUV the cart tipped and dumped my groceries into the slushy mess. The quickest way to recover my items was to open the back hatch and place them directly into the vehicle. So, I left my groceries in the slop and went to the rear of the SUV and pushed the unlock button. But it didn't work, so I went to the driver's side door, and pushed the button several more times. No luck.

I sloshed back to the tipped grocery cart, set it up, returned my dripping groceries, and pushed it closer to my vehicle. Then I remembered the SUV has keyless entry and I punched in the numbers. But I put in the numbers for the pickup truck not the SUV! Ugh! (Head slap here.) Now the vehicle is totally confused and no numbers will work.

Do you remember the TV show, *Are You Smarter Than a Fifth Grader*? This escapade should be called, *Are You Smarter Than Your Vehicle*. Holding the key in my hand, I resorted to old school philosophy and unlocked the door manually. Why didn't I think of this earlier? Smart decision, right? No—bad idea! Now the vehicle alarm is squawking and the headlights are flashing, alerting the entire parking lot that I am breaking and entering! I frantically push the alarm button on the key fob but it won't turn off the alarm because the battery is dead!

In a moment of panic, I did the only thing I could think to do. I put the key in the ignition and started the SUV, and just in case you ever have this problem, it works! (Though now I question the safety of the situation. If I unlock the door with the key and it sets off the alarm, why is it okay to start the vehicle with the same key?)

Thankfully I discovered a way out of my situation, and likewise the Holy Spirit will always provide a way out when temptation comes your way. In the passage below notice Paul says, **when** you are tempted, not if you are tempted. We are human, so temptation is inevitable, therefore God always shows us a way to remove ourselves from the temptation.

> *If you think you are standing strong, be careful not to fall. The temptations in your life are no different from what others experience. And God is faithful. He will not allow the temptation to be more than you can stand. When you are tempted, he will show you a way out so that you can endure. (1 Corinthians 10:12-13)*

All too often we cross the line when temptation comes our way and blame God for the fall. But just as my SUV alarm sounded, the Holy Spirit will set off an alarm of danger within us. At this point we have a choice to make. Flee even when it is difficult, or fall into temptation. God will provide a way out. We just need to request the strength and wisdom to select the correct path.

Our desire should be to live a righteous life. A life which is faithful and loving to others. One which also holds us accountable as we fellowship with other Christians. If our desire is for God to use us in mighty ways, we need to lead a clean and pure life. *(2 Timothy 2:20-22)*.

Regardless of how clean and pure we live; we still need God's grace. Without it, none of us will ever reach heaven because we all fall short of God's standard. *(Romans 3:23)*. What Paul says in *1 Corinthians 10:12-13* is don't abuse grace. Don't do whatever you want and then ask for forgiveness later. All too often, we repeatedly fall into the same sins. God provides a way out but it is our decision which avenue to follow.

For many, grace is a hard concept to grasp. The difference between striving to live a pure life and the gift of a pure life by grace. If you don't understand, just remember when temptation comes your way, God will always provide a way out. And no matter what choice you make, or how many times you fall, Christ also covers you with His grace when you ask forgiveness for your sin.

The Rock

This fall Jim and I moved a huge blue-gray rock from one of our fields to our yard. It was quite the process to load it onto the trailer. Jim shoved and turned, and turned and shoved with the tractor. I ran from side to side as I gave hand directions until he finally pushed it onto the dump trailer with just a couple of inches to spare on each side.

I hopped in the pickup truck and headed for home with squishy tires on the trailer from the heavy load. Jim followed behind in the tractor in case we had problems. I pulled in our driveway, parked and breathed a sigh of relief. I made it without a flat tire! We had only one attempt to put the rock in the perfect location. Once the trailer tipped the rock would be at its new home.

We both agreed on the location and I pulled the trailer forward to the side yard on the curves of our driveway. I reassessed the placement of the rock from every angle and finally gave Jim the thumbs up. He unlocked the trailer and pulled it off the trailer and into position with the tractor. I love the location and we did a great job of centering the rock in the side yard. Hopefully this spring I can get the guys to put my antique dinner bell beside the rock. I might plant a few flowers and add some mulch making a beautiful entrance to our home.

The rock reminds me of the old hymn, "My Hope Is Built on Nothing Less" where the chorus says: "On Christ, the solid rock, I stand. All other ground is sinking sand.[ix]"

When Edward Motes wrote the hymn, I wonder if he was referring to Jesus' parable about building your home on the solid foundation, the Rock? The words to the song are biblical and definitely convey the truths found in *Matthew 7*.

When Jesus told this parable, He didn't refer to a physical rock like the one we moved to our yard. He referred to the foundation upon which we are to build our Christian lives. In order for us to have a strong foundation, we need to have a strong relationship with Christ. If we simply have the attitude that Christ exists, but don't have a firm foundation or a solid rock relationship with Him, what will we rely on when problems come our way?

Christ gave us an example of a solid rock relationship with the Father when He prayed in the Garden of Gethsemane. Many pictures portray Christ as He kneels beside a rock and pours out the agony of his soul to God. Christ knew what was ahead of Him as he prayed. Betrayal. Torture. Humiliation. Pain. Agony. Death. But in spite of His anguish He prayed, *"I want your will to be done, not mine." (Matthew 26:39b).*

Christ asked Peter, James, and John to pray as well, but they couldn't stay awake. They couldn't stay alert and engaged in prayer with the Father for even an hour! Christ even reprimands Peter and tells him not to give into temptation and fall asleep again. Christ leaves and returns only to find them asleep once again!

You and I are no different than the disciples. We want to do what is right but we struggle with temptation. Just this morning as I prayed my mind drifted to other thoughts. I continually refocused on God and prayed again. Sometimes it takes discipline, focus, practice and strength to maintain a relationship with the Lord. But it is a necessary relationship so when difficulties come, we are connected to the Father.

When problems come my way and they will, I want to be able to stand upon the rock in our front yard, ring my dinner bell in praise and loudly proclaim, "On Christ the Solid Rock I stand. All other ground is sinking sand." When troubles come your way, I pray you too can claim these powerful words and remember The Rock upon which you stand!

Suggested Scripture Reading
- *Matthew 7:24-27*
- *Matthew 26:36-45*
- Look for scriptures which refer to God as the Rock

Lost Cell Phone

My husband, Jim, walked in the other day and said, "Don't you ever answer your phone?"

I began to flip papers and walk in circles as I looked for my phone. (You know...the frantic search because you have no clue where you left it.) As I headed for the backdoor, I said, "I never heard it ring it must still be in the car."

Just to be ornery he dialed my phone number on his phone with one hand, and answered my phone with the other hand. Apparently, my phone dropped out of my pocket earlier that morning—in the gravel by the shop where everyone parks! Fortunately, it has a purple case and he saw it before tragedy struck. (As my friend Deb would say, "Thank you Baby Jesus!") I on the other hand didn't even know it was lost.

I would like to say this is the first time my cell phone has gone missing but I walk around all the time asking, "Have you seen my phone?" My other question is "Has anyone seen a pair of my glasses?" One of the latest misplaced items is my change bag I use for book and craft shows! (If you want to search my house I will give you a reward when you find it.)

I don't know what my problem is but I misplace items constantly. I used to claim it was because I worked full-time and was raising two boys. Everyone feels as if those years are utter chaos. They are now grown, married, and have kids of their own. Then I claimed menopause as my excuse. We all struggle to keep it together throughout those times. Now? Well I don't want to say I'm old so I guess I will accept the fact I am just scatterbrained.

Honestly, it goes clear back to my childhood. I can remember many Sunday mornings when I was the family member who made us late for church because I couldn't find my dress shoes. One thing I do know, the busier I am the more stuff disappears! (Like the change bag. I was busy preparing for Thanksgiving dinner so I'm sure it's somewhere safe.)

We are blessed because God isn't scatterbrained like me! God is never so busy that He forgets where we are! He is always available, twenty-four hours a day, seven days a week, to answer our prayers. (If He had the need for a cell phone—He would follow us on social media, answer our emails, phone calls, and text messages too.) He cares for your every need because you are precious to Him. We can make our plans in life but God will lead us each step of the way. You are even so important to Him that He knows you by name.

Just like my cell phone was lost we are all lost in a world of sin. This amazing God who knows your name, cares for you, directs your steps, and answers your prayers, has one greater purpose in mind. He wants to rescue you and care for your soul.

> *For God saved us and called us to live a holy life. He did this, not because we deserved it, but because that was his plan from before the beginning of time—to show us his grace through Christ Jesus. And now he has made all of this plain to us by the appearing of Christ Jesus, our Savior. He broke the power of death and illuminated the way to life and immortality through the Good News. (2 Timothy 1:9-10)*

Allow this omnipotent, caring, loving and amazing Father rescue you from this sinful life. A life which sometimes makes you feel like a missing object. The reality is, you are of great importance and worthy of your Heavenly Father's love.

Suggested Scripture Reading
- *Exodus 33:17*
- *Psalm 65:1-5*
- *Proverbs 19:21*
- *Matthew 6:30*
- *Luke 12:7*

Shattered Window

We have a horizontal decorative window which is about eight feet long and one foot high above three vertical windows in our office. As I walked into the office one day, I noticed the window was shattered. I initially thought a bird hit the window, but the inside pane is the one broken. Therefore, the reason for the broken window remains a mystery.

The shattered pattern on the window looks like butterfly wings, without a body. It started almost exactly in the center of the window, and grew up and out into a beautiful pattern. Each time I enter the office, I look at the window. It is such a wonderful example of our shattered lives. Like the window, we are broken. Sometimes we feel as if our lives are shattered into hundreds or thousands of little pieces. Shattered marriages. Shattered families. Shattered health. Shattered churches. Shattered finances. So many broken pieces that we don't know how to put our lives back together again. But no matter how shattered we feel, God will turn our broken lives into beauty. He puts the pieces back together in a masterpiece which only He can create.

The pattern of the butterfly wings in the window reminds me of a new creation. *"This means that anyone who belongs to Christ has become a new person. The old life is gone; a new life has begun!" (2 Corinthians 5:17).* Christ takes all the pieces of your shattered life and makes you a new person. First comes the forgiveness of your sins. He changes you on the inside. You think and act differently because you are now guided by the Holy Spirit. Many people today say you are reformed or rehabilitated, but Christ says you are recreated. Like a butterfly who emerges from a cocoon, He takes those shattered pieces of your life and makes you into a beautiful person.

You no longer live a self-centered life. You now live for Christ as a new creation. *(2 Corinthians 5:15)*. A life where you begin to think and act more Christ-like. A life where God takes all of your shattered pieces and creates you into a beautiful person who lives for Christ.

As you walk this new journey with Christ, *"Let your roots grow down into him, and let your lives be built on him. Then your faith will grow strong in the truth you were taught, and you will overflow with thankfulness." (Colossians 2:7).*

Like our broken window, the reason for your brokenness may always be a mystery. You may never know why God allowed you to walk through such pain and suffering. But you can cling to His promises. God will turn your shattered life into a masterpiece. One which only a Sovereign God can create.

Suggested Scripture Reading
- *2 Corinthians 5:11-21*

Reflection

One day I found my granddaughter Reagan looking at her reflection in the dryer door. As is typical of a child her age, she smiled and pointed at herself enjoying the moment. She thought she was adorable and I tend to agree. What small child isn't adorable around the ages of two or three. They can be strong willed and stubborn throughout those "I do it" stages, but they also learn, grow and explore. I am inspired by their eagerness to discover and their mindset of I can do anything.

Somewhere between birth and adulthood, many adults lose focus of the mindset *"I can do all things through Christ who strengthens me." (Philippians 4:13 NKJV)*. We should follow the example of the toddlers, because they practice this verse every day even though they are unaware of its existence! The "I can't" mindset is prevalent for so many, for various reasons. Lack of desire to learn. Past failures. Harsh words. Poverty. Low self-esteem, just to name a few.

To overcome these hurdles in life, we need to focus on how Christ sees us. *Isaiah 62:4* says *"The Lord delights in you."* Just as Reagan delights in her own reflection, the Lord delights in you. He smiles and enjoys you—the wonderful person He created. Why does He smile and enjoy you? Because He loves you. *"See how very much our Father loves us, for he calls us his children." (1 John 3:1a)*.

Because God loves us and delights in us, He also wants us to grow in our Christian walks. This is where the "I can't" attitude needs converted into "I can." We claim we don't understand the Bible, therefore we don't read it. But we need to study and learn ourselves. We are challenged in *Hebrews 5:12a* to learn and grow as Christians. *"You have been believers so long now that you ought to be teaching others. Instead, you need someone to teach you again the basic things about God's word."* Dig into God's Word and allow it to bring back your *"I can do all things through Christ who strengthens me"* attitude. The more you study God's Word, the more you will see yourself as Christ sees you.

When we look in the mirror our humanness sees the flaws, the mistakes, the scars, and the unworthiness in our reflections. Though it is sometimes difficult, the reflection we should envision is the person Christ sees. Christ sees our beauty, our smiles, our knowledge, and our abilities. Just as I see Reagan as an adorable child, Christ sees us as His adorable children.

In his letter to the Corinthians, Paul admits the reflection we see here on earth is not the same reflection we will one day see in heaven. *"We don't yet see things clearly. We're squinting in a fog, peering through a mist. But it won't be long before the weather clears and the sun shines bright! We'll see it all then, see it all as clearly as God sees us, knowing him directly just as he knows us!"* (1 Corinthians 13:12 MSG).

In spite of this continual battle to see ourselves through God's eyes, He calls us to *"Trust steadily in God, hope unswervingly, love extravagantly."* (1 Corinthians 13:13b MSG). When you look at your reflection each morning remember God is delighted to see you! When you see yourself through God's eyes, you will find strength to love who you are in Christ. You will then be able to extravagantly love others.

Leah's Dedication

My mother-in-law, Leah, took great pride in attending all of her grandchildren's events. They spent their winters in Florida, but if she was in Ohio, she never missed a ballgame, a pig show, a band concert, or a choir performance. Even though she occasionally paid the price for her attendance, her dedication to her grandchildren was endless.

Jim often laughs about the time she was in a horrible mood for several days. He finally confronted her about her attitude, and she confessed she had received a speeding ticket on the way to her granddaughter's choir performance. She was clocked driving seventy miles per hour in a thirty-five mile per hour zone! She had never had a speeding ticket before and began to cry because her name would be printed in the local paper like a criminal.

My favorite story about Leah is the night I took her to my son's band concert. It was a cold, windy, rainy night, but she insisted that she attend. On my way to get her, I turned the seat warmer on low to warm her seat. After the concert, Ryan started my car and turned the seat warmer on but he left it on high. About one mile down the road Leah started squirming in her seat yelling, "Something's getting hot down here!"

I tried to explain how to turn off the seat warmer, but she couldn't find the button. She squirmed and wiggled in her seat the entire drive home. She survived her bun toasting incident and it makes me laugh every time I recall the episode.

In spite of her mishaps and funny stories, Leah was a dedicated lady. Her dedication to her family, friends, and God was evident in her life. When she passed away many years ago, we heard numerous stories of how she visited friends. She faithfully delivered her canned peaches, homemade applesauce, pies, frozen corn, corn on the cob, pickled beets, and such. She was on the go but none of us realized where she was going or what she was doing. She was thoughtful and caring to others as she lived out her life's mission to the fullest. Leah was not only dedicated to her grandchildren; she was dedicated to others. She spread God's love with her homemade treats and fresh produce which she shared with many friends.

Leah lived a life worthy of *Proverbs 3:3, "Never let loyalty and kindness leave you! Tie them around your neck as a reminder. Write them deep within your heart."* Her dedication to serve others and sow seeds of kindness was her life's goal. It didn't matter if it was friends or family, she was there. She cooked, canned, and baked to spread a little kindness to everyone. She wrote letters and sent care packages to college students. She even survived toasted buns and a speeding ticket to let her grandchildren know how much she loved them.

"Loyalty makes a person attractive." (Proverbs 19:22). Leah was attractive to her friends and family because of her loyalty and her love. Friends were delighted when she came to visit. Leah delivered her gifts with a smile, listened to their woes, and offered a heart full of kindness like no other.

Not everyone has the dedication to care for friends and family like Leah. I challenge you to find your niche in life, dedicate your talent to the Lord, and live your life to the fullest as you spread the love of Jesus to others.

Pelican

While basking in the sun on my brother-in-law's deck in Florida, I heard a huge splash in the canal, over and over again. I quickly learned the splash was from a brown pelican who was landing head first in the water. My first thought was God didn't give the pelican much grace if it has to land on its head. I read a bit about pelicans and discovered it was quite the opposite. God gave them great eye sight. They see the fish from the air and dive in after their dinner. Why land feet first if you can do a crash landing and have dinner at the same time! God gives the pelican the ability to dive into the water to catch fish even though it seems quite odd.

God orchestrated another oddity which we find in the book of Joshua. The walls around Jericho were a mighty fortress for the people who lived within, but God put an odd plan in place when He told Joshua to walk around the city for seven days.

The priests led the Israelites as they blew rams' horns and carried the Ark of the Lord around Jericho once a day, for six days. The Israelites didn't say a word. They didn't question God's motives. There were no arguments with Joshua about the strange details. They simply followed the instructions of the Lord. It was a huge step of faith when they circled Jericho seven times the last day. *"It was by faith that the people of Israel marched around Jericho for seven days, and the walls came crashing down." (Hebrew 11:30).*

The people inside the walls of Jericho (with the exception of Rahab) had to wonder why they blew their horns and circled each day. Yet at the same time, they feared the Israelites. There were rumors of how the Israelites continually conquered many lands. They probably shook in fear each day, and worried about the unknown. As the people of Jericho cowered in fear and confusion, God's plan went into action.

> *On the seventh day the Israelites got up at dawn and marched around the town as they had done before. But this time they went around the town seven times. The seventh time around, as the priests sounded the long blast on their horns, Joshua commanded the people, "Shout! For the Lord has given you the town!" When the people heard the sound of the rams' horns, they shouted as loud as they could. Suddenly, the walls of Jericho collapsed, and the Israelites charged straight into the town and captured it. (Joshua 6:15-16, 20)*

Just like the pelican, God sometimes has an odd way of caring for us. He gave the pelican the gift of eye sight and controlled crash landings as a source of nourishment. And as odd as this great plan of God's was for the Israelites to conquer Jericho, it was a mighty step in faith and a success. The Israelites allowed God to fight their battle for them. They didn't question His unusual plan, they simply circled Jericho in faith.

We too can trust God's blueprint for our lives. However unusual God's plan may seem, He is the One who knows exactly what we need to survive like the pelican and to thrive in the Promised Land like the Israelites.

Social Media

Last night I read an article about the ten practices which should be eliminated from the church. The writer felt sermons should be eliminated from the church service which totally shocked me. They compared the length of the sermon to the attention span of people as a result of social media. They didn't feel it was a valuable use of time and there were more effective ways to teach in today's society.

So, for all of the social media people who are reading this book here is your devotion for today. Please feel free to skip to the social media of your choice because apparently, time is of the essence and your attention span is limited.

TWITTER *Jesus wept-John 11:35* Lazarus died. Jesus felt compassion for Mary & Martha's loss and He cried. Reminded me of the loss of my mother. #JesusWept #Jesus #Lazarus #IMissMom

FACEBOOK *"Jesus wept." (John 11:35)*. So when Lazarus died, Jesus wept with the other mourners. I have never quite understood this scripture. I get the fact He was sad but why in the world would he cry! He knew He was about to raise Lazarus from the dead, so why cry? Seriously? I just don't understand. My BFF says Jesus had so much compassion for Martha and Mary over the loss of their brother, He cried. But it still doesn't make a bit of sense to me. Would you have cried if you were Jesus? After all, He knew Lazarus was about to be raised from the dead! It seriously CONFUSES me. If there were more than two words in this verse it would help me understand. Why didn't God give us more of an explanation? I want to understand this short verse.

What do you think FB friends? #JesusWept #Jesus #Lazarus #Confused #BibleConfusesMe #INeedAnswers.

INSTAGRAM Great verse. So much importance in two simple words. #JesusWept #Jesus #Lazarus

Photo by: Christine Lynn Photography

SNAPCHAT Sorry, you're too late the picture is already gone. However, you can find it on my **PINTEREST** account. Follow me at http://www.pinterest.com/MrsMaryRodman/pins/

Call me old fashioned but I love a good old sermon. One which convicts me, shares the gospel, and uses illustrations to which I can relate. It breaks my heart that social media is changing how we worship and how we teach the Bible. I have often joked *"Jesus wept"* is the easiest Bible verse to memorize but these two simple words are a power packed gem. It shows Jesus' compassion. His love for Martha, Mary and the other mourners.

He too loved Lazarus and felt a great loss. Maybe Jesus shed tears because He knew He was about to perform the greatest miracle of all time. A miracle, which was also His last recorded miracle in the gospel of John.

No matter what your social media preference, or if you don't follow social media at all, please don't miss this point—Jesus is a compassionate, loving, Savior. He sees your joy and your pain. He longs to celebrate with you and comfort you. When you smile, Jesus smiles. But when you weep, Jesus weeps. No matter how you feel today know Jesus understands your situation and your emotions because He too once walked this earth as a man.

Donnie

Later, Levi invited Jesus and his disciples to his home as dinner guests, along with many tax collectors and other disreputable sinners. (There were many people of this kind among Jesus' followers.) But when the teachers of religious law who were Pharisees saw him eating with tax collectors and other sinners, they asked his disciples, "Why does he eat with such scum?" When Jesus heard this, he told them, "Healthy people don't need a doctor—sick people do. I have come to call not those who think they are righteous, but those who know they are sinners." (Mark 2:15-17)

A few months ago, we received an unexpected message that our friend Donnie had passed away. The Lord called him home at the young age of fifty and you can truly say it rocked the community as the news spread. Donnie was an example of the scripture above. There were no good or bad people in Donnie's world. He shared many meals with people who might fall into the categories of *"tax collectors and disreputable sinners."* Donnie too once lived the life of a sinner and had fallen short, but by the grace of Jesus he changed his life. Plus, he changed without altering his association with others. And like Jesus he loved those who were considered disreputable sinners as much as he loved his family.

Donnie's son Billy wrote his dad's obituary and used these words to sum up his dad's life. "He was a man who never met a stranger; those who didn't know him knew of him and how truly great a man he was.ˣ"

As a John Deere salesman for Parrott Implement, Donnie impacted the lives of his customers and employees. He was not just a salesman; he was a counselor for many who sat in his office. He would always lend an ear in troubled times. Those who poured out their hearts knew without a shadow of a doubt their personal problems would never leave his office. Outside the office, Donnie was a family man, community member, and community leader. He was a coach and a silent witness as he loved everyone. The number of lives he touched became evident to his family as they greeted guests for nearly twelve hours at his calling hours.

Few of us can live up to Donnie's example of love and friendship, but we are all called to love like Jesus loves. *"We know how much God loves us, and we have put our trust in his love. God is love, and all who live in love live in God, and God lives in them. And as we live in God, our love grows more perfect."* (1 John 4:16-17a).

Each day we need to follow Donnie's example, live life to the fullest and love more. When we live by Donnie's mantra, and love the disreputable sinners our legacy will live on to impact our family, our friends, and our community.

Donnie's death though a tragedy and a shock has brought another friend to question the existence of Jesus and life after death. Our prayer is that one day he too will know Jesus and understand the difficult question which haunts him. His question—Why do bad things happen to good people?

In this case, Donnie's work on earth was done. His legacy lives on to impact the kingdom of heaven as we all strive to live a life like Donnie's, commendable of God's praises. Our goal should be to live a life worthy of the same greeting Donnie received when he met Jesus. As he reached heaven's gate, I see Jesus with His arms wide open as He said, *"Well done, my good and faithful servant."* (Matthew 25:21).

The Breeze

With my friend by my side,
Mexico, we did go!
To beaches far and wide,
And the sunshine aglow.

The sun's so refreshing,
A breeze in the air.
The waves, oh so soothing,
Relaxation, our share.

Burdens and tensions,
We left those behind.
With God's intervention,
This vacation's sublime.

Very soon we'll return,
To our home far away.
With a little less churn,
And there we will stay.

Oh, God has refreshed us,
Our spirit renewed.
A vacation with no fuss,
And scenery we viewed.

All thanks to our Savior,
For times such as these.
To rest in His favor,
And bask in His breeze.

Flea Market

While in Florida this winter, my brother-in-law was sure we didn't miss any of the local flea markets. It is funny how those who winter in Florida seem to be obsessed with this as a hobby. The first flea market seemed to be total junk, but today I found some treasures. All sorts of hair clips and bows, a neon tie dye lunch box, and a blue purse with hearts for my oldest granddaughters. I couldn't find a truck or tractor for Jackson, or a baby toy for Kennedy though. For myself I found reading glasses, a picture for the wall, and a necklace. Just like they say, one person's junk can be another person's treasure, especially at a Florida flea market! Though the value of my treasures was small the morning was fun and it provided entertainment.

Another way to have a fun morning is to find great treasures in God's Word. You know, those little gems you have read many times before but suddenly they take on a whole new meaning. For me yesterday it was, *"Take delight in the Lord, and he will give you your heart's desires." (Psalm 37:4).*

In his book, *But God: Changes Everything,* Herbert Cooper reminds us that we often focus on the second part of the verse. The part where we receive the desires of our heart but we skip our part which is to delight in the Lord. Cooper goes on to say,

> *"Please understand that the word delight is not just a synonym for happy. I believe it refers to joy. If you 'take delight' in the Lord, this means you take 'great pleasure' in the Lord. You enjoy spending time getting closer to God through the*

Word and in prayer and these things don't feel like tasks to you.[xi]"

Herbert's words echoed in my mind as I drifted off to sleep last night. I have never considered it a task to dig into God's Word or spend time in prayer, yet life often gets in the way. I don't want to be a church goer, devotion writer, conference speaker, who barely scratches the surface of the true depth of knowledge in God's Word. In order for me to dig deeper and learn more, I need to carve out a special time with God on a daily basis.

I am thankful for authors like Cooper who have been blessed with the ability to teach others, and share their knowledge in wonderful books with great biblical insight. I have no biblical degree, my devotions simply come from the school of hard knocks as I look for God in my everyday life. I'm not bashing of my own books but I also urge you to allow yourself time to read more than my devotional each day. Pick up a good Christian book which digs into a topic of interest, or focuses on a specific book of the Bible. For today, maybe just allow yourself to read the Bible wherever it opens and concentrate on a verse or two to obtain better knowledge. Ask God to reveal the meaning of those little gems you might have previously overlooked. And please, remember to spend time in prayer each day so you may delight in the Lord.

A true Snowbird or Floridian enjoys a great flea market. A true Christian wants to grow closer to God and spend time each day in prayer and study so *"He will give you your heart's desires."*

Bottle of Wine

While in Mexico with my friend Angie our tour group warned us not to drink the water or beverages made with the water. We simply could not drink one more diet pop, so we ordered wine for dinner. We stayed at an all-inclusive resort which included wine and alcoholic beverages. Our mistake was that we didn't say *house* wine. Before we understood the problem, the cork was popped on a bottle of wine and we were told it would be charged to our room! Neither of us enjoyed our meal, (except for the crème brûlée) because we were worried about the cost of the bottle of wine.

Following dinner, I was handed a receipt to sign for our sixty-five-dollar bottle of wine and was told to add a tip! (It was a no tip resort.) We were somewhat relieved and upset all at the same time. We had visions of the wine costing much more, yet it was an expensive bottle of wine by our standards! Through conversations the next day, we discovered others had been tricked and it was the most expensive wine on their wine menu. A menu which we never even saw. I'm not a wine connoisseur, but I'm sure it wasn't worth thirty-two-fifty a glass! The waiter turned our innocent request for two glasses of wine into a gimmick and an expensive purchase.

We later joked about how to tell my husband about the sixty-five-dollar bottle of wine which was charged to our credit card. I mean, how do you start the conversation?

"Oh by the way honey, we purchased a bottle of wine at dinner last night. You will see it on the credit card bill."

"I thought wine was included at the resort. Was it good?"

"Well sort of. Did I forget to mention it cost us sixty-five dollars?"

I'm not saying our glass of wine with dinner was sinful by any means. However, the trick the waiter played on us was sinful. He had a way about him which hid the truth. As a waiter in a resort he knew guests typically meant house wine when they ordered. He took advantage of the situation and conned us into an expensive purchase. His choice of words through a language barrier was very deceptive. We indicated we didn't want a whole bottle of wine just one glass each, but he was quick to show us the cork had already been popped.

When it comes to sin, Satan too can be just as sly, tricky and deceptive as our waiter. He makes sin look pretty, enjoyable, and pleasurable. Even the simple sins which draw us in, such as "sharing in love" when it is truly gossip. Those little white lies to cover a spending problem. When boredom strikes or a stressful moment comes your way, you eat the fattening comfort food which totally ruins your diet. Maybe you flirt with a married co-worker or neighbor, and the relationship begins to escalate. We are all guilty of sin. No one can avoid it. Even Jesus was tempted. The difference between us and Jesus is that He never gave in to sin. *(Hebrews 4:15)*. We cannot combat sin on our own and neither did Jesus. He battled sin with the Word of God. We not only have the Word but we also have the power of the Holy Spirit.

> *If you think you are standing strong, be careful not to fall. The temptations in your life are no different from what others experience. And God is faithful. He will not allow the temptation to be more than you can stand. When you are tempted, he will show you a way out so that you can endure. (1 Corinthians 10:12-13)*

God always provides a way out; we need to listen to the Holy Spirit and step away from the temptation. Quote a scripture and say a prayer asking God for help. Remember how easily we were tricked into a sixty-five-dollar bottle of wine by a waiter? Well Satan is the master of temptation and evil. Walk away. Walk away from the gossip circle. Walk away from the stores and online purchases. Walk away from the junk food. Walk away from the sinful relationship. No matter what your temptation, walk away, and walk into the arms of Jesus.

Deception

As the Israelites began to claim the promised land word quickly spread throughout Canaan of their success. Those who lived in the area were aware the battle wasn't just with Joshua and his men; the battle was against the Lord's army. As a result, many kings banded together to form a stronger resistance as the Israelites moved closer to their territories.

But the Gibeonites took a different approach. They felt it was better to become servants to the Israelites than to be annihilated like Ai and Jericho were. So, they sent a group of ambassadors out to greet the Israelites. They had them wear old tattered clothes and worn out sandals. Among their possessions were split wineskins and moldy bread. They did an excellent job of portraying men who were tired and weary. The deception continued as they told Joshua and his men they had traveled a great distance when actually they had not traveled far at all. The leaders questioned the men from Gibeon as to their motives, yet by all appearances their story checked out.

> *So the Israelites examined their food, but they did not consult the Lord. Then Joshua made a peace treaty with them and guaranteed their safety, and the leaders of the community ratified their agreement with a binding oath. (Joshua 9:14-15)*

Just as the scripture says, all too often we forget to consult the Lord on the small decisions in our lives. We are much more likely to consult God when we face a huge battle or a major decision. But on those simple, easy decisions in life, we seldom take the time to seek His will.

Joshua always sought the Lord's guidance before he went to battle. This one time, their story appeared to be so true and innocent, why bother the Lord? His decision to make a treaty with them had horrible results!

The Israelites found themselves in quite a predicament. Joshua and the leaders had sworn an oath in the presence of the Lord and they were not happy about the peace treaty. But if they broke the oath, they would have to deal with the wrath of God. The Israelites made the best of a bad decision and made the Gibeonites their woodcutters and water carriers.

While I read the story of how the Gibeonites deceived Joshua, I reflected upon my own life. There have been both good and bad decisions over the years. I can recall the time Jim and I purchased some of our first farm ground and our home. A great deal of prayer took place prior to each purchase. When we were financially strapped in those first years after the purchase, God always provided exactly what we needed. I can't imagine a major step in my life without God's guidance.

The opposite scenario, we did not pray about the purchase of a small SUV. We barely drove it a year because it was not right for our family. Oh, what a financial mistake we made on a whim with a little persuasion from a salesman! We were deceived just like Joshua.

No matter where you are in your Christian walk, a new comer to the faith, or a well-seasoned Christian, we all have times when we forget to consult the Lord in our daily lives. Joshua was no exception, and he fell into the trap of the Gibeonites. My best advice is to walk through life a little slower and don't make hasty decisions. Learn from Joshua's mistake and consult the Lord in all your decisions so you will not be deceived by others.

What's Your Handicap?

I have written about my father a lot in this book, but he is a great father and has taught me so much. In a previous devotion, I mentioned Dad was a church going, God fearing, hard-working man. What I didn't mention is he lost his left arm years ago in a farm accident. He was only twenty-seven years old at the time and married with three children.

I have never considered Dad a handicapped person. He never made a big deal about the situation or considered the loss of his arm a burden. It was just part of his life and as kids we considered him normal like everyone else. Granted some tasks are more difficult for him, like buttering his bread. It tends to move across the plate since he can't hold it down. Usually someone will notice and lend a hand. (No pun intended.) But on the flip side Dad always said, "I can't smash my thumb when I drive a nail because I hold the nail with my hook." What an asset!

Not only has Dad overcome his handicap, he took advantage of the situation. He worked with the prosthetic engineer to make it useful for him on the farm. Dad could have allowed the accident to change his life and his career choice, but he chose to overcome his handicap to succeed on the farm.

We all have handicaps in our lives. Not necessarily physical ones, but handicaps which prevent us from serving God. Our handicaps can also change based on our situations. Five years ago, my biggest handicaps were fear and procrastination. I thought, "I don't have time to put those devotions into a book. Besides, what if I publish a book and no one likes it?" Overcoming that fear became my biggest asset. I am overwhelmed with blessings from *Bloom Where You're Planted.* What is my biggest handicap today? Marketing knowledge. God has turned my book into a ministry. I see the potential ahead of me, but I lack the marketing knowledge to move forward and succeed. So how do you and I overcome our handicaps?

First start with the scriptures. Find a biblical story, an example, or verses to conquer your handicap. My favorite verse to tackle fear is *Isaiah 41:10*. Procrastination can be overcome when you focus on *Proverbs 13:4*. If you wonder where I will find marketing knowledge in the Bible, I'm not sure. But I can find wisdom. *"If you need wisdom, ask our generous God, and he will give it to you. He will not rebuke you for asking." (James 1:5)*. Wisdom from God is exactly what I need every step of the way as I overcome my handicap.

So, what's your handicap? What do you plan to do about it? If you turned to this devotion for the answer, you looked in the wrong place. I can offer examples and suggest scriptures, but to overcome your own handicap, you have to do the work yourself. Just as Dad worked with the prosthetic engineer to turn his prosthesis into an asset for farm life, you have to turn your handicap into an asset in your own life.

I suggest you start with the advice in *James 1:5*. Take your Bible in hand, use the concordance or an online resource such as www.biblegateway.com [xii] and search for wisdom! Great wisdom can be found in the book of Proverbs. Strength can often be found in the Psalms. Many biblical people overcame their handicaps to serve God. Moses was a Hebrew raised as an Egyptian. Handicap or asset? Joseph was sold into slavery and later saved the Jewish people from starvation. Handicap or asset? And I love impetuous Peter. He walked on water and then he sank. He later boasted he wouldn't deny Christ, yet he did. Handicap or asset?

Regardless of your handicap in life, you have a choice to make. You can allow it to stop you from serving the Lord or you can turn it into your greatest asset. Dad's handicap became one of his biggest assets in life. Like no more smashed thumbs! He overcame any and all obstacles set before him. And truth be known, he can actually butter his own bread it just takes a little extra work.

God blesses our lives each and every day. Download a free pdf file, **Blessings**, created from my devotional, *Bloom Where You're Planted*. It is available at www.MaryRodman.com/BookBonuses. My Peanut Butter Fluff Pie recipe is included, so bless your family and friends with a delicious dessert!

Give Everything

Sunday in church my husband gave me an elbow nudge and pointed for me to watch the two small girls in the front. The girls are cousins and probably twelve to eighteen months old. The older of the two took the pacifier out of her mouth and offered it to her cousin, who gladly accepted the gift and put it in her mouth. The mother removed the pacifier and returned it to the oldest girl. Even though the parents tried to stop her, she continually shared her pacifier with her friend.

At a young age, a pacifier can be your world, your security and your comfort. It is the one item you just can't live without. It was so cute to watch her give up **everything** so willingly for her cousin. *"A friend loves at all times." (Proverbs 17:17a NIV).* and this little girl was loving with all she had to offer—her pacifier.

How often are we a reflection of *Proverbs 17:17*? Do we show unconditional love to our family, our friends and our neighbors? Most of us would have to admit we do not. The world has tainted our view of who is lovable, who is precious, and whether or not they deserve unconditional love. Love can make such an impact on a person's life which is why *1 Corinthians 13:13* says, *"the greatest of these is love."*

I recently heard a statistic which supports this fact. Approximately sixty percent of the men released from prison will return again one day. Yet only about ten percent of those who have attended a Kairos weekend while incarcerated, will return to prison. Kairos is a Christian prison ministry which shares the love of Jesus with the inmates. The inmates who participate in the weekend are shown unconditional love. The love doesn't end once the weekend is complete either. The Kairos team frequently returns to the prison to show their love and have Christian fellowship with the inmates. What a testimony and witness to the gospel of Christ.

The disciples gave up everything and committed their lives to following Christ. They left behind family, friends and careers to follow and learn from Jesus. Yet after Christ's death and resurrection, they returned to the only activity they knew—fishing on the Sea of Galilee. Simon Peter even said *"I'm going fishing." (John 21:3)*. It was as if he said, "Christ isn't here anymore so what else is there to do but fish. Are you coming with me or not?" So, they climbed in the boat, fished all night and caught no fish.

Once again, Christ steps in and teaches one last lesson. He tells them to cast their nets on the other side of the boat and instantly the nets overflowed. He prepares them breakfast and then he challenges Peter one last time by repeatedly asking, *"Simon son of John do you love me?"*

"Yes Lord, you know I love you," Peter replied.

"Then feed my sheep," Jesus said.

It was as if Jesus said, "Why in the world are you guys fishing? Your vacation is over. Get busy and get to work. Love on these people and share the gospel! I gave up **everything** so you and others can have eternal life. Now go teach them!"

How about you? Are you willing to share your pacifier, the object which means the world to you, with your best friend? Most likely. But will you share the gospel with a neighbor? Could you commit to love those in prison so they might have a better life after they are released? God called the disciples to give up everything, to love the unlovable, and to lay down their lives for the sake of the gospel. He also calls you and I to do the same because *"There is no greater love than to lay down one's life for one's friends." (John 15:13)*.

Suggested Scripture Reading
- *John 21:1-17*

Raindrop

When I was in elementary or middle school, I had to write a creative story for an English project. It was to be written as if I was an inanimate object. I didn't quite understand the assignment, so my sister Janet suggested I write the essay as if I were a raindrop. My initial thought was big deal, a drop of rain falls from the sky, and soaks into the ground. What a dull story.

But when I wrote this story, it became one of the defining moments in my life. It opened my mind to creative thinking. I wrote as if I was a drop of water which came from the sky in a downpour of rain. I was swept away by the rush of the water as I floated down a ditch. Then somehow, I was rushed back up through the garden hose which had a sprinkler attached. As I flew back into the air, I was excited to return to the freedom of the sky.

I no longer have the story, but the memory is still vivid in my mind. The story of the raindrop is just one of many defining moments in my life. Those moments when something good or bad shapes you into the person you are today. Often, we forget about these events, or even see them as insignificant. At such a young age, I never expected this story about a raindrop to lead to my creativity and my love to write and tell my stories.

We have good and bad defining moments in our lives and sometimes those moments happen close together. The woman caught in the act of adultery had two defining moments in a matter of minutes. As a result, her life was changed forever.

It is apparent that the woman caught in adultery had low self-worth as she lived a promiscuous lifestyle. She didn't hide her act of adultery in the dark of the night. She was caught and dragged out into the street in the middle of the day. She was brought out as a sinner who deserved death, in front of a large crowd of people, and Jesus. The law said both parties should have been stoned yet the Pharisees only pointed their fingers at this woman. They found great pleasure humiliating her in front Jesus and the group of onlookers.

Not only was she caught in the act of adultery, but the Pharisees used her like a pawn in a game. Their objective had nothing to do with her. They wanted to trap Jesus. I envision her on the ground, curled up in a ball in an attempt to cover herself and the shame she felt as people stared at her. All the sins in her life were suddenly exposed to a large crowd, in a public place, and before this man named Jesus.

The Pharisees asked Jesus for permission to stone her and demanded an answer. I find it fascinating that Jesus doesn't answer them right away. As if to ignore their demands, He stoops down and begins to write in the sand. What did He write? Was it a message to the woman? Was there scripture written in the sand which caused the Pharisees to have a change of heart?

Bible scholars offer different opinions as to what Jesus wrote in the sand. Some say He wrote scripture to convict the Pharisees. Others say He wrote the names of her accusers in the sand. My favorite speculation is He actually wrote the word forgiveness, because He was about to teach the true meaning of forgiveness. Forgiving others and forgiving ourselves.

Jesus finally stands up and gives them permission to stone her and says, *"All right, but let the one who has never sinned throw the first stone!" (John 8:7b).* Can you imagine how this woman cowered in fear at this moment! Maybe her arms were above her head as she anticipated the stones about to hit her. But nothing happens! Jesus bends down and writes in the sand once again. Maybe this time Jesus actually wrote the names her accusers who overlooked their own sins. Slowly, one by one, the Pharisees all turned and walked away, with the oldest and wisest of them leaving first.

"Only Jesus was left in the middle of the crowd with the woman. Then Jesus stood up again and said to the woman, 'Where are your accusers? Didn't even one of them condemn you?' 'No, Lord,' she said. And Jesus said, 'Neither do I. Go and sin no more.'" (John 8:9b-11).

Talk about your defining moments. In a series of a few minutes this woman had two great defining moments. The first one was the moment she was dragged out into public, and put on display for all to see, exposed and humiliated. The second one was the instant Jesus said, *"Neither do I. Go and sin no more." (John 8:11b).*

The woman caught in adultery had a decision to make. She could return to her promiscuous life style, or she could choose freedom through the forgiveness of Christ. Likewise, we all have good and bad defining moments in our lives. But are bad defining moments truly bad when Christ uses them to change us?

Email Blunder

This week I struggled to accomplish numerous goals. I felt as if a stopwatch clicked from the moment I rose until I crawled into bed. High on my list of priorities was to submit a book proposal which I had worked on the prior week. This required internet access and of course our internet bounced on and off like a lively rubber ball all day.

I finally had a moment when it appeared stable, so I started my submission email again. Then I accidentally pushed send without the attachment. I searched for the email in the sent folder and it wasn't there. Assuming it was a bad internet connection, I breathed a sigh of relief because I didn't actually send the message. I started a new email and made a wise decision to attach my file first. I copied in my generic message and pushed send. I was horrified as the email flashed off the screen. I forgot to change 'Dear Mr. XX' to 'Dear Joyce'! It was sent—gone—swirling through cyber world headed to its destination.

To add to my stress, remember the first email? Throughout all of the internet problems, I had mistakenly logged into my old email account. My first email had sent—gone—swirling through cyber world headed to its destination as well. Joyce was about to receive two emails, from two different accounts and neither one of them was correct! I realized this wasn't a good day to send emails and felt it best not to attempt a third email to apologize for the blunder.

How could I have possibly made such a mess of this important email? Instantly I was upset and angry at myself. Would she even look at my proposal when I created such a blunder? Failure is exactly what raced through my mind all day. In spite of my mistake I tried to remind myself God is in control of every situation, even email blunders.

There was a time in Peter's life when he felt like a total blunder too. After the Last Supper, Jesus told the disciples they would soon scatter and deny they ever knew Him. But Peter denies the accusation. He even brags in front of the other disciples. *"Even if everyone else deserts you, I never will." (Mark 14:29).*

But Christ warns him again, *"I tell you the truth, Peter— this very night, before the rooster crows twice, you will deny three times that you even know me." (Mark 14:30).*

Jesus is soon arrested and His predictions come true. Peter denies knowing Christ three times in the courtyard. As the rooster crowed the second time, *"Jesus' words flashed through Peter's mind: 'Before the rooster crows twice, you will deny three times that you even know me.' And he broke down and wept." (Mark 14:72b).*

This beloved disciple of Jesus was no different than you and me. We all have moments of failure, whether big or small in our lives. Peter's mistake was huge but life is full of choices. Peter made the choice to forgive himself and continue to follow Christ. He went on to preach the gospel to a large crowd on the day of Pentecost and was instrumental in starting the Christian church.

I too had a choice to make. I could continue to see myself as a failure or see the humor of the situation. When I think about what Joyce received on the other end of cyber world, I have to laugh. A nicely written email addressed to her, but no attachment. A few minutes later she receives the same nicely written email addressed to Mr. XX, with the attachment, and from two different email accounts! She probably wondered who is this nut case on the other end of cyber world and do I want to even look at her proposal!

Regardless of the hobbled mess of emails, I did receive a reply from Joyce. Though she was not able to help me at this time, she did give me some sound advice and encouragement. I am forever grateful because encouragement is just what I needed to hear after my blunder.

What a great reminder that our sovereign God has our lives under control. From the day of Pentecost to email blunders, He will always mend our hearts, forgive our failures, and cover us with His unending love.

Glitter Stones

My son spray-painted bedroom decorations for his girls in their drive-way. Now you can find stones which were over-sprayed with pink and purple glitter paint. His youngest daughter Reagan picked up a couple of the pink stones and brought them to my house. Bless her heart what a precious gift. Grandma's never dispose of their grandchildren's prized gifts so now they sit near my computer as a reminder of her kindness.

The stones are pretty, smooth, shiny and neon pink on one side, but the flip side is rough and ugly gray limestone. One stone makes a slow transition from gray to pink glitter as it gradually changes into a beautiful stone. We are much like these stones which now adorn my desk. Without Christ our lives are rough, ugly, gray and lack purpose. Without the joy of the Lord we have no reason to be a bright shining light. But when we allow Christ into every part of our being, we make a slow transition from gray to glitter as Jesus Christ transforms us into a new person. It then becomes our responsibility to spread the gospel and share how our lives with Christ bring us pure joy.

> *You're here to be light, bringing out the God-colors in the world. God is not a secret to be kept. We're going public with this, as public as a city on a hill. If I make you light-bearers, you don't think I'm going to hide you under a bucket, do you? I'm putting you on a light stand. Now that I've put you there on a hilltop, on a light stand—shine! Keep open house; be generous with your lives. By opening up to others, you'll prompt*

people to open up with God, this generous Father in heaven. (Matthew 5:14-16 MSG)

Jesus calls us to be the salt and light to the world. It is our responsibility to share the gospel and a responsibility we should take seriously. Don't hide what Jesus has done for you. Share it with everyone you encounter. We all have a faith story to share. A moment when the Lord comforted us or a time when we felt Christ's presence in our lives. Share it! Tell the world! Be a witness of His greatness to those who desperately need to hear the gospel of Christ. Don't do it because you feel you have to—do it because you want to be a glittery neon light shining in a lost world.

Wild Flowers

Years ago, when we lived at the old farm house I enjoyed countless walks to the creek behind the barn. It was a quiet beautiful place to pray and just contemplate life. Spring was my favorite time of year there, because the purple, white, and yellow wildflowers were in bloom. Some years it was absolutely breathtaking. Even though they only bloomed for a few weeks, I enjoyed the flowers as much as possible.

Then one year, my father-in-law sprayed weed killer up and down the creek bank from his 4-wheeler. He didn't just hit weeds here and there. No, he sprayed the entire creek bed and killed almost all of the beautiful flowers! My heart was broken. What was once a beautiful place to sit and pray, became desolate. It was many years before the wildflowers began to repopulate and it may never be as beautiful as before. So, my memory of beautiful walks by the creek will always be just a memory.

Just as my father-in-law attempted to kill the wild flowers, Satan tries to kill our hopes and dreams. He distracts us in numerous ways. Worldly turmoil. Wayward children. Illnesses. Business problems. Finances. Many various problems can disrupt our day to day lives and squelch our hopes. But we always have victory in the Lord. When we have a small glimmer of faith in God it sustains us in our Christian lives. Just like a few wildflowers repopulate the creek bank, hope in the Lord repopulates our spirit each day.

Isaiah lived during turbulent times. The Assyrians constantly attacked Judah, causing the people of Judah to live in constant fear of invasion. Even though this powerful enemy was persistent Isaiah encouraged the people to have hope in the Lord.

Make the Lord of Heaven's Armies holy in your life.
He is the one you should fear.
He is the one who should make you tremble.
Preserve the teaching of God;
entrust his instructions to those who follow me.
I will wait for the Lord,
who has turned away from the descendants of Jacob.
*I will put my **hope** in him.*
(Isaiah 8:13, 16, 17 - Emphasis added)

Isaiah continues to speak to the people of Judah and challenge them. They can either turn toward mediums, and psychics who seek advice from the dead, or they can put their hope in the true living God. They were blaming their problems on God, rather than accepting the fact that they had walked away from the one true God who had rescued them time and time again.

We need to follow in the footsteps of Isaiah and find hope in the Lord. When we have hope in the Lord, we have hope in our lives. So why not seek the Lord to calm our fears and ask Him for guidance. We are privileged to have the Bible in multiple versions, languages, along with electronic access today. There is no excuse for not reading the scriptures for our daily source of hope!

I hope one day the wild flowers will repopulate from the weed killer disaster and be as beautiful as before. And I pray life will not crush your spirit as you find daily hope in God's Word.

Lord, sustain me as you promised, that I may
live! Do not let my hope be crushed.
(Psalm 119:116)

In the Year 2525

While listening to an oldies radio station I heard the song *In the Year 2525*. I chuckled as I remembered a Christmas day from my childhood. Not to tell my age but this was the era of 45 records. (If you are too young to understand Google it.) On this particular Christmas, my sister requested this song on a 45 record and she was excited to receive it.

I don't recall the details of the day but I do remember the moment Mom heard the words to the song! Prior to Janet spinning her new record Mom was clueless about the song. If you aren't familiar with the lyrics, they portray a bleak outlook on the future of mankind and question the existence of God. Mom was unhappy with her daughter for requesting such music and upset she had purchased this horrible song.

The day is vivid to me because Mom and Dad seldom had disagreements but one was about to ensue. I wouldn't say they argued but Dad definitely didn't have the same concerns about the music as Mom. Dad calmed her down and the day remained joyous. They even allowed the Christmas present to stay in our home.

Even though the song was written about the glim outlook of mankind it didn't influence Janet or myself in any way throughout our teen years. However, Mom did have legitimate concerns from a biblical standpoint. As people, or in this case as teenagers, we are what we listen to, what we read, and what we watch on television. Satan loves to work his way into our lives and manipulate us through subtle exposure to non-Christian venues.

For example, if you are surrounded by others who use foul language you will soon find yourself repeating those same words. When you surround yourself with temptations such pornography, alcohol, sex and drugs, you are often tempted to travel down a similar path of destruction.

On the other hand, when you do life together with other Christians you hold one another accountable. Paul speaks of this accountability to the people of Galatia. He urges them to help those who have gone astray and gently lead them back to Christ without sinking into temptation (*Galatians 6:1)*. We are called to help each other lead a godly life.

> *Don't be misled—you cannot mock the justice of God. You will always harvest what you plant. Those who live only to satisfy their own sinful nature will harvest decay and death from that sinful nature. But those who live to please the Spirit will harvest everlasting life from the Spirit. So let's not get tired of doing what is good. At just the right time we will reap a harvest of blessing if we don't give up. Therefore, whenever we have the opportunity, we should do good to everyone—especially to those in the family of faith. (Galatians 6:7-10)*

The Christian life can be difficult when walked alone. God calls us to work together and hold one another accountable to make our lives easier. If a friend turns away from Christ don't allow them to walk away. Gently and humbly lead them back to the Father and a life filled with grace. After all, one day it could be you who strays away from Christ and needs a humble gentle friend to lead you back on the straight and narrow path of grace.

Out on A Limb

"Get out on a limb! You see the fruit's not around the tree trunk, it's out on the edge of the limb."
John Maxwell[xiii]

This quote is accredited to numerous people, with slightly different versions. My personal favorite is John Maxwell's because he explicitly describes why you can't live your life hugging the tree. I don't know if my sister-in-law Lori ever heard these words throughout her lifetime. However, Lori lived her life to the fullest as if she had been told to *"get out on a limb!"*

As a young mother, it was Lori's home where all of the local children flocked to play. The kids always knew that if they went to her house with their friends, the day would be new and sensational. It wasn't about the latest games or toys; it was about the adventures Lori created. Indoors, outdoors, off to a park or a store. No matter the destination it was always a fun and exciting day.

As an artistic person, Lori was never afraid to learn a new craft, take up a new hobby, or try a new recipe. Gardening. Painting. Interior design. Remodeling. Quilting. Cooking. Lori was a master of all and much more. She truly found her niche as a painter, and created beautiful pictures many of which her family knew little about. She also designed a quilt from her own imagination to reflect her love of the beach near their Florida home. Her creativity was endless.

She possessed a humble giving spirit as well. She gave of her time, her abilities, her smile and her laughter. She quietly and humbly devoted her life to family and friends. She asked nothing in return, because that is exactly what you do when you *"get out on a limb"* and live your life for others.

Lori's humble spirit continued throughout her battle with colon cancer. She seldom indicated that she was in pain, and requested people not make a big deal about her illness. Her goal was to live each day to the fullest, which she did. She cherished her family and her friends, and was especially proud to be a grandma. She would often show pictures and videos of her only granddaughter, Hadley, and smile and giggle with excitement.

I don't know if Lori had a favorite scripture which she leaned on for strength throughout her cancer battle. But as a fellow believer, I can imagine her leaning heavily on the words in this passage.

> *I pray that from his glorious, unlimited resources he will empower you with inner strength through his Spirit. Then Christ will make his home in your hearts as you trust in him. Your roots will grow down into God's love and keep you strong. And may you have the power to understand, as all God's people should, how wide, how long, how high, and how deep his love is. May you experience the love of Christ, though it is too great to understand fully. Then you will be made complete with all the fullness of life and power that comes from God. (Ephesian 3:16-19)*

Lori's ability to live life out on a limb came from a deep trust in the Lord. God blessed her with a creative mind and spirit. From the home where the kids gathered to play, to being a grandma, Lori lived each moment for others with a humble spirit and kind words until the Lord called her home.

People like Lori are trend setters for those who are not as adventuresome. Occasionally we long to be more like those who take a risk, or go on an adventure, to fulfill their dreams. Our lives on this earth are like a flash of lightening compared to eternity in heaven. So why not fulfill the dreams God has put on your heart? Take a leap of faith, crawl away from the tree trunk, get out on a limb, reach for the fruit, and start living your life for Christ!

Thunder

While recovering from major surgery I had a day of setback. My pain seemed different and more painful than previous days. As if the pain wasn't enough to dampen my spirits it was a dreary morning. There was very little sunshine which eventually lead to pop-up thunderstorms in our area. Though the storms and rain weren't close the gloomy gray sky was above as the thunder rumbled in the distance for what seemed like hours.

I needed some sort of pick me up and grabbed my Bible to see what I could read about the thunder. There are verses which say God's voice resounds like thunder and others that refer to the thunder of the seas. Many verses speak of thunder throughout the end times in book Revelation but the scripture where I found encouragement for my pain was in *Psalm 77* which was written by Asaph.

I didn't know who Asaph was so I did a little more research. Asaph was believed to have been the director of music at King David's Tent of Meeting and at Solomon's temple. He was very much aware of King David's and King Solomon's ups and downs in life and knew about God's abounding love and forgiveness.

In the first half of the Psalm Asaph pours out his heart to God in despair.

> *Has the Lord rejected me forever?*
> *Will he never again be kind to me?*
> *Is his unfailing love gone forever?*
> *Have his promises permanently failed?*
> *(Psalm 77:7-8)*

Though these aren't the exact thoughts in my mind I have lamented and prayed similar words asking God to lift the pain so I can function normally again. As I continued to read the Psalm, I was reminded God is with me until I am totally healed.

> *But then I recall all you have done, O Lord;*
> *I remember your wonderful deeds of long ago.*
> *They are constantly in my thoughts.*
> *I cannot stop thinking about your mighty works.*
> *(Psalm 77:11-12)*

The Psalmist goes on to describe God's mighty power as He parted the Red Sea for the Israelites.

> *Your thunder roared from the whirlwind;*
> *the lightning lit up the world!*
> *The earth trembled and shook.*
> *Your road led through the sea,*
> *your pathway through the mighty waters—*
> *a pathway no one knew was there!*
> *You led your people along that road like a flock of sheep,*
> *with Moses and Aaron as their shepherds.*
> *(Psalm 77:18-20)*

Asaph started the psalm as if God was a distant part of his past, but he suddenly remembered God never leaves His people. He recalls the story of God's great miracle passed down for generations. God is still the God of great miracles today. What a wonderful reminder for me.

No matter how gray the skies may be, how much the thunder rolls, or even how much pain we experience in our lives, God is always there. Sadly, we are the ones who walk away from God when our needs are the greatest. We often experience moments of despair like Asaph and need to remind ourselves—if God can part the waters of the Red Sea, He can definitely send us thunder as a reminder of His greatness.

Killdeer

It is wheat harvest and time to bale straw on the farm. One of the fields is back a dead-end road, so there is little or no traffic most days. The killdeer birds have taken advantage of the lack of traffic and built their nests along the edge of the road. With every pass of a pickup truck, semi-truck, or farm equipment, the killdeers do their familiar killdeer call and hobble along like they have broken wings drawing our attention away from their nests.

I love the instincts God gave these small creatures. They will do everything possible to get us to follow them so we won't find their nests or babies. They risk their own lives, for the sake of their offspring when a predator is near.

God made so many wonderful creatures, and each one is unique. After each creation, God reflected and He said, *"It is good."* But on the last day God created man differently. We were created in His image.

> *So God created man in His own image; in the image of God He created him; male and female He created them. Then God blessed them, and God said to them, "Be fruitful and multiply; fill the earth and subdue it; have dominion over the fish of the sea, over the birds of the air, and over every living thing that moves on the earth." Then God saw everything that He had made, and indeed it was very good. (Genesis 1:27, 28, 31a NKJV)*

God created us to have fellowship with Him. He put within us a soul and a desire to thirst for more of His presence. A hunger to seek a relationship with Him. All too often we search for happiness in all the wrong places. The peace for our souls and joy for our hearts can't be found in material objects. Try as we might, they just don't satisfy a soul which desperately longs for God. Of everything God created, we are the most unique, because we have a soul. What an amazing creation we are!

God gave the killdeer birds the gift of drama as a means of protection. They are the best little imitators of a wounded bird you will ever watch. But God gave us protection also—The Holy Spirit—to guard us against evil. *"But when the Father sends the Advocate as my representative—that is, the Holy Spirit—he will teach you everything and will remind you of everything I have told you." (John 14:26).*

God loves us so much that He gave us the Ultimate Protector. No other creation on earth was given this option, except for mankind. The gift of the Holy Spirit is ours when we repent of our sins and believe in Jesus Christ as our Savior. Once we establish this relationship, the Holy Spirit will serve as our Protector and Guide all the days of our lives.

The decision is yours and it is plain and simple. You can try to protect yourself like the killdeer birds as you flap your broken wings and squawk for attention, or you can take the easy route and allow the Holy Spirit to fill your heart and guide your steps all the days of your life.

Abundance

Before you read this devotion, grab your Bible and read about the poor widow woman in *2 Kings 4:1-7.*

Every summer we bale a lot of straw on our farm and it takes a great deal of extra help. A typical day is anywhere from five to ten people on the crew. My primary job is to provide good meals, cold drinks and shuttle people from farm to farm when necessary. I forget from year to year just how much food it requires to feed all the men two meals a day! I serve everything from cold cut sandwiches to huge casserole dishes. And I bake cookies—chocolate chip, oatmeal raisin, snickerdoodles, brownies—lots and lots of cookies. I receive the highest compliments from everyone on the crew, and I joke that they come for the food not the pay check.

In the story of the poor widow, she is being forced to sell her sons into slavery to pay her debts. Instead of selling them, she asked Elisha for help. She didn't hesitate when Elisha told her to gather as many jars as possible from her neighbors and friends. Then she took a step of faith and began to fill all the jars. God multiplied the oil as it flowed from the flask until all of the jars were full! Not a single one was left empty.

God recently provided for me in a similar fashion. Wheat harvest was early this year and it caught me off guard. I was not quite up to par following my surgery, plus I had a lot of men to feed the first day. I had a moment of panic due to the lack of food in our house. I went to my small garden box to see if there were any green beans I could pick. There were plenty for a meal and I put them in the crock pot along with some potatoes and bacon. Once again, everyone raved about the food and especially the fresh green beans!

It seems like the more beans I picked this week, the more they produced. And then the zucchini started to produce in abundance too! We had green beans, zucchini casserole and zucchini bread for the entire straw season. God provided wonderful nourishment for all the men who helped bale the straw, and I was blessed with an abundance of vegetables when I needed them most.

As I picked green beans again last night, I thought about the poor widow woman Elisha helped. She continually poured olive oil from her flask into the jars until they were all full. I have picked and picked and picked again. I only have two short rows of green beans and I have fed the crew green beans three or four times in a week!

The olive oil was all the widow had left to survive, but God provided more than enough. The first night the green beans in the garden were all I had to offer as a vegetable and God provided. But God continued to produce the food I needed each day to prepare meals. The poor widow and I have one blessing in common, our needs were abundantly met by God. You too can have your needs met each day by God. Don't limit your blessings with a lack of faith, instead take a leap of faith and trust God. He will do immeasurably more than you can imagine!

> *Now all glory to God, who is able, through his mighty power at work within us, to accomplish infinitely more than we might ask or think. Glory to him in the church and in Christ Jesus through all generations forever and ever! Amen. (Ephesians 3:20-21)*

Dirty Truck

I jumped in the farm truck with my husband the other day as he asked, "Did you notice my clean truck?"

"Nope, can't say that I did."

"I had the guys clean it too while they were here working."

I smiled and said, "Well they forgot to clean the inside."

Then came *the look* because I did not acknowledge his shiny red truck. His farm truck is always dirty on the inside. It is used daily and typically for dirty jobs. Often the windows are left down when it is parked in the field, which allows the dirt to drift in and settle on the inside. Oh, the dashboard what a mess—filled with hats and papers, more hats and small tools, clipboards, and dirty rags, and more hats. (Yes, I counted 4 hats on his dash.) And remember all those items on the dash are covered in dust because the windows were left down. Greasy, oily objects and muddy boots often hit the floor boards and leave their marks behind as well. The seats, oh my goodness! He does have seat covers which helps, but remember it is the transportation for dirty men in dirty clothes to and from work. So, praise the Lord for seat covers to catch the dirt. But for today (and hopefully a few more days), the outside of Jim's farm truck is shiny bright red again!

Our lives are no different. We often live behind a façade of perfectionism on the outside, when in reality our souls are in turmoil. When we mask the pain of our inadequacies, we paint a picture to our family and friends of a beautiful life. Maybe the family next door is impressed with your car, your home and your beautiful landscape, but they have no clue that you struggle financially as a result. Depression may haunt you in the dark of the night, but while at the office you paint a picture of great joy and happiness with a fake smile. Some days you just long to be real. Real with others. Real with yourself. And especially real with Jesus. Many of us were taught to be perfect, while others placed perfectionism upon ourselves. When you attempt to live a perfect life, it can be exhausting. Christ doesn't want you to be perfect. He wants you to be real.

The Pharisees and the Sadducees also lived behind a façade of perfectionism and Jesus continually reprimanded them. They followed their man-made rules closely and were critical of others who didn't measure up to their standards. They made no exception for Jesus either, as they continually disagreed with His ways. To others, they came across as clean and perfect on the outside, but Jesus looked at their hearts and considered them disgraceful. They had Biblical knowledge, yet they alienated others with their hypocritical attitudes, laws, and perfectionism. They totally missed the definition of unconditional love which made them dirty on the inside!

The Bible tells of two members of the high council who were unlike the others. When Jesus spoke, they were drawn to Him and His message of love. While other members of the high council tried to manipulate and trap Jesus, they wanted to know more about this grace of which He spoke. They were so drawn to Jesus they took a risk to be seen with Him and believed in Him.

Nicodemus, was drawn to Jesus in the dark of the night. He heard Jesus preach and wanted to know more about this gift of salvation. Pursuing Jesus at night shows there was risk involved, yet he willingly came to Jesus and said, *"Rabbi, we all know that God has sent you to teach us. Your miraculous signs are evidence that God is with you." (John 3:2b).* He no longer wanted to hide behind the rules of perfectionism, he desired to know the real Savior and His endless grace.

"Joseph of Arimathea took a risk and went to Pilate and asked for Jesus' body. (Joseph was an honored member of the high council, and he was waiting for the Kingdom of God to

come.)" (Mark 15:43). Joseph was most likely a Pharisee or a Sadducee. Although he was a member of the high council, he was a secret follower of Christ. Jesus was his Lord and he took a risk by giving Him a proper burial.

We also need to take a risk and let go of our perfectionism. When we try to be the perfect Christian, with the perfect self-image, or have the perfect family, or the perfect marriage, we leave no room for Christ in our lives. Let us do away with the façade we live behind and take a risk like Nicodemus and Joseph and leave our perfectionism at the foot of the cross.

Tough Love

Sometimes in our lives we exhibit tough love to a friend or family member. Tough love is the moment you give another adult an ultimatum as a result of their bad actions. Tough love is a two-way street though. Your offer for help may be accepted, or it may be rejected. If the person continues down the wrong road, you must rely on the power of prayer and seek understanding from God. Now that is truly tough love!

My friend is at this crossroad in her life. Her son was recently picked up for drug possession. Will her son accept her invitation for help or will he continue to walk down his destructive path? Unfortunately, I have no great words of wisdom for her. The only words I have to offer are those written about Jesus when He exhibited tough love.

> *It was nearly time for the Jewish Passover celebration, so Jesus went to Jerusalem. In the Temple area he saw merchants selling cattle, sheep, and doves for sacrifices; he also saw dealers at tables exchanging foreign money. Jesus made a whip from some ropes and chased them all out of the Temple. He drove out the sheep and cattle, scattered the money changers' coins over the floor, and turned over their tables. Then, going over to the people who sold doves, he told them, "Get these things out of here. Stop turning my Father's house into a marketplace!" (John 2:13-16)*

Even though Jesus was angry about the Temple being used as a market place, He took time to braid a whip. In those moments, I wonder what went through His mind? Possibly He paused to see if the merchants would flee on their own, or maybe He needed time to pray before He cleared the temple. Regardless, it is obvious Jesus is about to make a profound statement and take a righteous stand against the evil practices in the Temple. When Jesus braided the rope, He sent a clear message for us to control our tempers and develop patience before we react.

In those moments when we exhibit tough love, we should always first braid a rope. Anger is typically our first emotion and angry words often cause more damage than good. Even though Jesus cleared the temple, He did so with righteous indignation. Tough love should be the same. In the case of drug addiction, we need to stand firm in a loving manner. We cannot display a gray and fuzzy line on what is permissible and what is not. Their lives are at stake, and we are the ones who stand in the gap between addiction and a godly path. We want what is best for our loved ones. In their mental state, they want the drugs which mask their failures, their pain and their inadequacies in life.

Even in Jesus' case, tough love did not work the first time. In the book of John, Jesus cleared the Temple at the beginning of His ministry. Almost three years later, Jesus cleared the temple once again as His ministry comes to an end. Jesus took one last stand, one last example of tough love for the abuse of the Temple. But ultimately, He won because His death, burial, and resurrection offered grace to all of those who He chased from the temple.

Many will continue down the path of addiction and destruction, rather than accepting your love and trusting God. Regardless of the outcome, trust is the key word for redemption. Trust that your tough love is necessary. Trust in the principle of braiding your whip. Trust in the prayers on their behalf. Trust in God's strength in the moment. Trust in God's timing that a story of redemption and victory will one day prevail.

Zucchíní Crísp

If you have ever grown zucchini in a garden you know one plant can feed one hundred, and four plants may feed five thousand. Fortunately, we only have one plant but the zucchinis are piling up in the fridge. In an attempt to get ahead of production, I made a zucchini supper. Zucchini and chicken casserole, which tasted a great deal like chicken parmesan. Zucchini bread, very similar to beer batter bread and it tasted great with the casserole. And for dessert we had zucchini crisp, which is where I took a risk and created the recipe myself.

I had a recipe for zucchini pie, but I didn't have a pie crust. (Confession here—I don't make homemade pie crust even though I'm a country girl.) Zucchini pie tastes just like apple pie, so I thought why not make zucchini crisp. I looked at several apple crisp recipes and combined ideas. A few more modifications to the spices, and I put it in the oven to bake. It was a little too sweet, but the outcome was delicious and with some minor sugar adjustments to the recipe, it will be better the next time.

We all need to take a risk in our lives from time to time. There are never perfect conditions, perfect opportunities, a perfect church, or a perfect time to sow seeds of faith. It is our responsibility to take a risk and seize the opportunity. We need to allow ourselves to be vulnerable, but at the same time, take a leap of faith and trust God. Solomon even tells us that life involves risks.

Send your grain across the seas,
and in time, profits will flow back to you.
But divide your investments among many places,
for you do not know what risks might lie ahead.

When clouds are heavy, the rains come down.
Whether a tree falls north or south, it stays where it falls.

Farmers who wait for perfect weather never plant.
If they watch every cloud, they never harvest.

Just as you cannot understand the path of the wind
or the mystery of a tiny baby growing in its mother's womb.
So you cannot understand the activity of God, who does all things.

Plant your seed in the morning and keep busy all afternoon,
for you don't know if profit will come from one activity or another—or maybe both.
(Ecclesiastes 11:1-6)

Solomon gives us great advice. He teaches us to take a risk on the uncertainties of life and have faith in God. We need to seize the possibilities and allow God to show us the profits of our work.

Jesus had no problem taking a risk when He fed the five thousand, and He did so without zucchini! I took a risk and create a new recipe, Zucchini Crisp. And for a lady who doesn't make homemade pie crust, this was a leap of faith. But on a bigger scale, I have always found it exciting to take a risk when serving Jesus. He has never let me down. There have been times of discouragement, but Christ always sends friends to encourage me when I need them the most. There have also been moments of deep study where God leads me to new and different scriptures to provide strength for the journey. And when it comes to decisions Solomon's words are always helpful.

I pray you take a risk today, whether it is a journey you are currently on or a new one which lies ahead. When you serve the Lord with a renewed faith, He will meet you every time.

Zucchini Crisp

6 cups Zucchini - sliced
1 ½ teaspoons Cream of Tartar
1 Tablespoon Lemon Juice
½ teaspoon Apple Spice
1-2 Tablespoons instant Tapioca
1 cup Sugar

Peel and remove seeds from zucchini. Cut into slices, similar to apple slices. Simmer for 10 minutes in enough water to keep from sticking. Drain well. Mix with the ingredients listed above and pour into a greased baking dish.

<u>Topping</u>
¾ cup Flour
¾ cup Instant Oatmeal
¾ cup Brown Sugar
½ cup Butter, softened
½ teaspoon Apple Spice

Mix all topping ingredients together and sprinkle on top of the zucchini mixture. Bake approximately 40 minutes at 350 degrees or until zucchini are tender and topping is crisp.

Take a risk and serve with love as you witness about Jesus!

Dullbozer

My son Ryan, his children, and I were on our way to the zoo when Jackson spotted a bulldozer out his window. With great excitement Jackson exclaimed, "Dullbozer Daddy! Look a dullbozer!"

"Yes buddy, it is a bulldozer," Ryan replied

The excitement in Jackson's voice was so cute. Even though we were headed to the zoo, Jackson would have been content to stay and watch the dullbozer instead. He inherited his love for trucks, tractors, and anything which moves from his daddy, so his excitement gave me a chuckle.

Jackson expressed great enthusiasm about the bulldozer, even though he couldn't pronounce it properly. Likewise, we should be eager to know and memorize God's Word. We may be able to recite scriptures word for word, like *John 3:16* or *Psalm 23*. Other times, we may only know part of a verse, or the connotation behind it. Whether we are great biblical scholars or baby Christians, we need to continually be in God's Word.

It is crucial to know God's Word for multiple reasons. First and foremost, to fight temptation. When Jesus was tempted in the desert for forty days, He fought Satan by quoting scripture. Scripture knowledge is also useful when we witness about Christ to others. I have often used scripture to provide comfort or advice for a loved one facing difficult situations. Moses even challenged the Israelites to memorize the Ten Commandments for their own benefit.

> *Take to heart all the words of warning I have given you today. Pass them on as a command to your children so they will obey every word of*

> *these instructions. These instructions are not empty words—they are your life! By obeying them you will enjoy a long life in the land you will occupy when you cross the Jordan River. (Deuteronomy 32:46-47)*

Moses didn't have the ten commandments on handouts for thousands of people wandering in the desert. They had to rely on repetition, memorization, and listening to every word from the prophets to know God's Word. We are blessed today with numerous Bible translations, study guides, and online resources. In some ways, it has spoiled us because we no longer need to memorize the scripture, we can look it up. Yet James reinforces the message from Moses.

> *So get rid of all the filth and evil in your lives, and humbly accept the word God has planted in your hearts, for it has the power to save your souls. (James 1:21)*

God doesn't expect perfection from you, not even when it comes to scripture memorization. What He desires is for you to stay in the Word and continually learn more scriptures. Sometimes they might come out a little twisted like dullbozer and other times they will actually be the correct words. The important part is to be in God's Word daily, hide it in your heart, memorize it, and pass it down to your children.

One day Jackson will be able to say bulldozer correctly. And as Christians our goal is to know more than the first key verse we typically memorize, *"For God so loved the world, that he gave his only begotten Son, that whosoever believeth in him should not perish, but have everlasting life." (John 3:16 KJV).* Why not join me and memorize *James 1:21* today?

Snuggles

After a trip to the zoo, my youngest granddaughter Kennedy curled up in my arms to rest. She had fallen asleep on the way home and was now in a daydream state, where toddlers are half awake and half asleep. She was nestled up on my shoulder and periodically opened her eyes, smiled with sleepy eyes, and drifted asleep once again. I knew snuggle days would soon end, and enjoyed every moment as I held her close. Eventually she woke, snuggled only a few more moments and slid off my lap ready for the next adventure.

When a child is snuggled in your arms, you feel a closeness you simply cannot explain. The warmth of their love as you hold them tight. Sometimes it is a big hug to assure them that they are okay, or like Kennedy maybe it is a sweet smile as they begin to awaken. Regardless of the reason for the snuggle, the result is the same. A bond is formed as two lives are filled with love for one another.

Throughout His ministry, Jesus also loved to snuggle with the children and bless them. He felt their warmth and love just as we do today, but He also used the children to teach us about His love.

> *The people brought children to Jesus, hoping he might touch them. The disciples shooed them off. But Jesus was irate and let them know it: "Don't push these children away. Don't ever get between them and me. These children are at the very center of life in the kingdom. Mark this: Unless you accept God's kingdom in the simplicity of a child, you'll never get in." Then, gathering the*

children up in his arms, he laid his hands of blessing on them. (Mark 10:13-16 MSG)

"*These children are at the very center of life in the kingdom.*" Not only is Jesus referring to the children He blessed, He also refers to us. We are God's children and He longs to be close to us. Even with all of our adult sins, adult questions, and adult problems, God desires to hold us in His loving arms of grace and bring us into His kingdom.

As adults, it is often hard for us to accept the love of Christ with a childlike faith. We bring judgment upon our own sinful lives as we wonder, "How could Jesus possibly love a sinner like me?" Maybe the scars of life make you feel empty, instead of loved. Jesus doesn't see your sins, Jesus sees you, the uniquely made, warm, lovable person He created. He longs to heal your brokenness and your pain.

Life can be a mystery, one we don't always understand, and you may ask, "How can grace be this simple?" The gift of grace is free, so take a childlike leap of faith, and gather into His affectionate arms of grace today. In your Savior's arms, you will find forgiveness for your sins, comfort for your broken heart, and peace for life's journey.

Close your eyes and rest in quiet fellowship with the King of Kings. Envision yourself snuggled beside Jesus, then smile and look into His loving eyes. No words are necessary, simply allow His arms of grace to comfort you as a bond is formed between you and Jesus.

Leap of Faith

My friend Dee is one of those behind the scenes people. When I worked as an administrative assistant at the church, she faithfully folded bulletins week after week. Few people at the church knew she did this for years. She was a reliable and faithful behind the scenes servant for Jesus. Dee is the type of person who will do any job you ask of her as long as it is behind the scenes—or so she thought.

I was organizing a one-day ladies retreat for our church and asked Dee to be the MC for the day. It took much persuasion on my part and a lot of prayer on Dee's part, but she finally agreed. My slight push to send her flying out of the nest was almost more than she could fathom. She was nervous about her role as MC and asked me to write her a script, so I did. She returned the next week she said, "I can't read this script. It just isn't me."

I was elated to hear her say this and replied, "I don't want you to read my script. I want you to be you which is exactly why I asked you to MC the day. You are perfect for the job. You are witty, creative, and you speak from your heart."

When one of the speakers shared her story at the event, she touched Dee's heart deeply. As a result, Dee shared her impromptu testimony! She had a faith story hidden deep in her soul and it bubbled out as she expressed her love and passion for Jesus.

I'm not saying everyone with the gift of helps can do what Dee did that day. I am saying—never underestimate the power of the Holy Spirit when you take a leap of faith. I challenge you to get outside your comfort zone to serve Christ. He will do amazing works through you when you simply meet the challenge.

Dee continually said no but God said yes and she listened. With God by her side Dee discovered she was capable of much more than folding bulletins. The more Dee trusts Jesus the more she loves Jesus. When first approached, she felt unworthy to be the MC. In the end, she touched more lives with her impromptu story than the speakers who prepared for weeks. Dee has journeyed through a rough childhood and an abusive marriage and finally into the arms of Jesus. She now knows that she is a chosen, precious, and beloved child of God.

Dee built her faith through prayer, Bible studies, support groups, and God's Word. I encourage you to search the scriptures to increase your faith today. Where will you find strength? Possibly in the faith chapter of *Hebrews 11*, or maybe in a small Bible story where someone insignificant took a leap of faith to draw closer to Jesus.

Artesia Geyser

While on vacation, we spent a couple of days in Yellowstone National Park. Since we have been there numerous times, we didn't see any of the main attractions. Instead we spent our time searching for wildlife, enjoying the mountain scenery, and a few of the less noted attractions. At one of those stops, I discovered the Artesia Geyser. It was a small geyser yet I found it to be absolutely remarkable.

Artesia Geyser is named appropriately, as the word artesian means a constant flow of water from underground. This geyser continually emits water. It spews water close to the ground non-stop, and then about every minute or two, water shoots in the opposite direction about five feet high. Slowly the water level goes back down to about a foot off the ground again. A continual pattern of up and down, high and low, which never ceases. When the water shoots high into the air it is beautiful as it faithfully repeats its pattern.

God too is like the Artesia Geyser. His love continually flows to us. There may be moments when we feel God is distant, like the tiny spew of water from the geyser. Other times, we feel His great love and warmth like the beautiful Artesia Geyser as it spews water high into the air. God's love is real and around us every day. Nothing can stop God's great love for His people.

> *And I am convinced that nothing can ever separate us from God's love. Neither death nor life, neither angels nor demons, neither our fears for today nor our worries about tomorrow—not even the powers of hell can separate us from God's love. No power in the sky above or in the earth below—indeed, nothing in all creation will*

ever be able to separate us from the love of God that is revealed in Christ Jesus our Lord. (Romans 8:38-39)

Artesia Geyser, Yellowstone National Park

The Move

Well today is the day. We are moving Dad into an assisted living facility. I can't say he is resisting, but he definitely isn't excited about the change either.

For roughly the first fifty years of my life, Dad was my number one advisor. I could ask his advice and he would freely give an answer. Slowly this has changed, and now if I ask for advice, he no longer shares words of wisdom. The tables have turned, so my siblings and I are now making decisions for him. As difficult as it may be, it is all part of the cycle of life.

My sister persuaded Dad that it was the right choice to move to assisted living by simply asking Dad to trust her. Our family was raised to trust one another, so Dad graciously accepted the decision to move. We trusted Dad's wonderful advice for so many years and now it is Dad's turn to trust us.

This is a heart wrenching day since Dad has lived in his home for fifty-seven years. He raised his family here on the farm. He has enjoyed his grandkids here and watched them become wonderful adults. Now he loves to see the great-grandkids and give them gummy worms for treats. Fortunately, none of this enjoyment will change, there will just be a new normal. A new place to visit Dad, or Grandpa Joe as he is affectionately called by all the great-grandchildren.

As I reflect back over the years, where did we learn to trust one another. Honestly, Dad never gave us bad advice which was where it all began. But trust runs much deeper than within our home. Throughout his life, Dad built countless relationships based on his ability to trust others. In other words, trust was the root of his entire life.

When I search the scriptures, I find a more gratifying definition of the word trust. Paul pleads with the Roman church to trust one another. The church was a diverse group of people. Jews and Gentiles. Rich and poor. Slaves and free people. With all of this diversity it was difficult for them to trust one another, but Paul urged them to love as Jesus loves. He encouraged them to pray together, share meals together and to avoid favoritism. For the church to grow and the gospel to spread, they had to find common ground and love one another. Paul continued his encouragement as he taught them God was their source of hope.

> *I pray that God, the source of hope, will fill you completely with joy and peace because you trust in him. Then you will overflow with confident hope through the power of the Holy Spirit. (Romans 15:13)*

I am thankful for Paul's words of encouragement, and the reminder that Christ Jesus is our source of hope. For us to be responsible for Dad's wellbeing requires a deep trust in the facility and the staff. As a family, we have to trust one another as we make this decision for Dad. So, the cycle of life continues, with trust as our foundation.

Yet today is the day. The day I was able to finish this devotion. I was overcome with emotion when we moved Dad. I was unable to put my thoughts to paper, so I put this devotion aside after four short paragraphs. Many months have passed and trust is still the key to Dad's lifestyle change and his adjustment to his new home.

No matter how difficult the decision, Dad required more assistance than we could offer. He trusted us and made the transition. He continually trusts all of the new people who surround him. The reliable staff, who lovingly assists him with his daily needs. His friends and family who come visit and help him adjust. And like the Roman church, his new friends come from different walks of life. They have joined together in fellowship and hope as they trust one another. But the greatest blessing of all is the trust Dad has given us, his children, to make a great life choice on his behalf.

Combine Repair

Just a few days into fall harvest our combine broke down. It wasn't until the repairman took the it apart that he found the actual problem. There was a factory defect deep inside the machine which was not obvious from the outside. I wish it was a simple repair but unfortunately it was not.

From all appearances, you would not know the combine was inoperable. It is only a couple of years old, the engine runs great, and it is still a shiny John Deere green on the outside. But somewhere deep within there was a serious mechanical problem. In order for the repairman to find the problem, they had to remove the entire backend of the machine. All of those parts are now strewn across the floor of our shop. Since the problem was considered a factory defect, we are fortunate the repairs will be covered by warranty. (Praise the Lord for good news!)

In many ways, we are like the combine. If we have a broken arm or leg on the outside, it is obvious to those around us that we have been injured. Likewise, with the combine you can see if something is broken or bent on the outside. But you can't judge the condition of a combine by its appearance. Only the operator knows when there is a mechanical failure deep inside. Such is the case with us. By all outward appearances, we may look great on the outside but only our Operator, God, knows we are broken on the inside.

We age gracefully and so does the combine. The combine will lose its green luster as the paint begins to dull from the sun. It will begin to need repairs here and there as parts become worn. Through the years, we too slowly become grayer, and wrinkles begin to appear as we age. We have our aches and pains, and some people even get new parts, such as knees and hips.

We often put more emphasis on our outward appearance than we do our inside condition. Slowly as time passes our brokenness may trickle out in various emotions, unless we take care for our soul. Occasionally we need to unload all of our broken "parts" on the floor before the Lord and allow Him to do a great repair.

> *For the word of God is alive and powerful. It is sharper than the sharpest two-edged sword, cutting between soul and spirit, between joint and marrow. It exposes our innermost thoughts and desires. Nothing in all creation is hidden from God. Everything is naked and exposed before his eyes, and he is the one to whom we are accountable. (Hebrews 4:12-13)*

We cannot hide our brokenness from Christ. He already knows our heartaches, our regrets, our challenges, our struggles, and our thoughts. At times, we may not feel God's presence, but He is still there. But there is good news. We too are covered by God's warranty for life! When we lay our "parts" before the Lord and seek healing in the Word of God, our lives will become whole once again. Some of our problems are small repairs, while others seem insurmountable. It is throughout these insurmountable ordeals God will surround us, comfort us, and put all of our "parts" back together as He repairs our souls.

Underfoot

Underfoot is a beautiful calico cat, but she is also unique. About half way up her tail takes a turn similar to a cork screw and then continues on. It never seems to bother her and the veterinarian said it is most likely a birth defect. She was very tame and healthy when abandoned on our farm. Due to her friendliness, she was always underfoot when the men were unloading semi-trucks full of grain, thus her name. This unique cat not only has a corkscrew tail and an unusual name, but she was also an orphan.

Eventually my son Matt decided to take her into their home. Now she spends her days lounging in the shelter of their house away from the farm traffic. When Matt chose to provide Underfoot protection, it was a wise choice. Small kittens and heavy farm equipment are never a good combination, especially when they are friendly and desire attention like Underfoot.

Just as Matt provided shelter for Underfoot, all throughout scripture God commands us to provide for those who are less fortunate, particularly the widows and orphans. *Psalm 146:9* says, *"He cares for the orphans and widows."* God has the ability to come down from heaven, build them a shelter and provide them with nourishment, but He doesn't. He calls upon us as Christians to do so.

In today's fast paced world with internet capabilities, we live in a "me" society far from the concerns of those less fortunate. But throughout the Bible, God continually reminds us to put the needs of others first. *"Pure and genuine religion in the sight of God the Father means caring for orphans and widows in their distress and refusing to let the world corrupt you." (James 1:27).*

James continues to challenge us to put our faith into action. In other words, walk the walk, not just talk the talk. *"What good is it, dear brothers and sisters, if you say you have faith but don't show it by your actions? Can that kind of faith save anyone?" (James 2:14).* One way to put your faith into action is to provide shelter for the widows and orphans of this world. This can be accomplished in numerous ways. Worldwide charity organization. Food banks. Homeless shelters. Recreation Centers. The list is endless.

When we choose to care for those who are less fortunate, God will bless our lives. Matt chose to care for Underfoot and she has blessed their lives greatly. Underfoot has also taught his daughters responsibility and compassion for God's creatures. If God can bless their lives with a rescued kitten, how much more will He bless our lives when we show true devotion to the oppressed, the homeless, and the unsaved.

"God blesses those who are merciful, for they will be shown mercy." (Matthew 5:7). May your actions reflect the love of Jesus today and may God bless you as a result.

Suggested Scripture Reading
- *Matthew 5:1-11*
- *James 1 and 2*

Dale

Many years ago, my nephew Dale was born extremely handicapped. Among his handicaps was the inability to see or speak, to crawl, or even sit up without support. As he grew older and with the help of therapy, he was able to do simple tasks like turn the dial on his musical toy, or bring food to his mouth. As he grew the muscles in his body began to cause further discomfort as his hips and spine began to twist.

The doctors said he would never live past the age of three or four, but we were blessed to have Dale in our lives for fourteen years. In spite of his handicaps, he was the most delightful boy. There were times when he would grunt or groan and even grind his teeth. I'm sure in those moments he experienced some pain, which he was unable to communicate, but he seldom cried. My fondest memory of Dale was his laughter. He would laugh when you spoke to him, or pushed his wheel chair ever so gently back and forth. His greatest laughter came at the sound of his favorite musical toys, or when his mom would speak to him and love on him. Some might consider raising Dale a burden, but we considered it an act of love. Even though it was hard work for his parents, the blessings far outweighed the time spent to meet his daily needs.

Many people suffer from handicaps in this broken world. Not just physical handicaps either. Some suffer with the handicaps of mental illness or learning disabilities. Like Dale many have physical handicaps from birth or as a result of an accident. Some cannot see while others are unable to hear. We are all handicapped in one way or another and when we acknowledge our handicaps, we allow Christ to work through our weaknesses. *(2 Corinthians 12:9)*.

Among those who suffered handicaps in biblical times was Mephibosheth, who was the son of Jonathon, and the grandson of Saul. At the age of five, Mephibosheth's nurse was rushing to save his life and fell injuring his feet. *(2 Samuel 4:4)*. David promised Jonathon he would always show kindness to his descendants and requested Mephibosheth be brought into his home. David had no apprehensions about Mephibosheth's handicap or his inabilities, he only had compassion for him.

Mephibosheth was afraid to visit the king and bowed low before King David as a servant, but David assured him he had no intention of harming him and said:

> *"Don't be afraid! I intend to show kindness to you because of my promise to your father, Jonathan. I will give you all the property that once belonged to your grandfather Saul, and you will eat here with me at the king's table!" Mephibosheth bowed respectfully and exclaimed, "Who is your servant, that you should show such kindness to a dead dog like me!" (2 Samuel 9:7-8)*

Due to his crippled body, Mephibosheth felt unworthy to be in the presence of the King. King David on the other hand showed love and mercy as he restored Mephibosheth's rightful inheritance. Mephibosheth no longer had to worry about his handicap or his inability to provide for his family. He lived the rest of his days under the care of King David.

This Old Testament story is a wonderful foreshadowing of Christ's invitation to us. We are all handicapped broken sinners. No matter what our brokenness may be, God invites us to the table of forgiveness. Salvation isn't for the perfect or those who appear sinless. Salvation is for all, no matter our disability. When we come to the table of forgiveness, we too can live the remainder of our days and know the King of Kings cares for us.

God cares for the handicapped people on this earth. Whether it is physical handicap like Dale's, or the disability found in our own spiritual weakness. Dale's handicap wouldn't allow him to speak or talk to Jesus in an audible way. But Dale loved music which included the great hymns of the church. He praised the Lord all the days of his earthly life as he smiled and laughed to the music, and now he praises Jesus in heaven.

God calls you to lay down your handicap and come to the table of forgiveness. Won't you join Mephibosheth and Dale at the King's table of forgiveness today.

Difficult Decisions

There are times in our lives when we face difficult decisions. Sometimes we choose correctly, and sometimes we don't. Once we realize we made a bad decision, all we can do is learn from our mistake and move forward to correct the direction. Every decision in our lives is like a fork in the road. If you turn to the left and it is the wrong direction, you need to turn around and go to the right and correct the problem. The most important part of our journey is to learn from our mistakes and gain wisdom along the way.

I also believe bad decisions, aren't always bad. (If you recently made a bad decision in your life, you are probably flailing your arms and ready to argue with me, but hear me out first.) If we live a perfect life and never make a bad choice, would we seek the Lord as much? Would we lean on Him for comfort? Would we rely on Christ for wisdom? For me, I know the more bewildered I am, or the more confused I become over decisions in my life, the closer I pull into Christ. It may be the need for forgiveness, or simply a desire for wisdom which brings me to the Lord in prayer. Therefore, I don't feel that a bad decision, is always bad. And trust me, I have made more than my share over a lifetime.

The Israelites continually made bad decisions throughout the years. Joshua reminds them that God has faithfully rescued them for many generations, in spite of their lack of faith.

Not only did God rescue them from slavery in Egypt, He parted the Red Sea so they could cross to safety. He fed them manna as they wandered in the wilderness for years. He even provided quail for them to eat because they whined about the manna. Joshua even pointed out that the Lord won each battle as they drove out their enemies and conquered the Promised Land. The Israelites had made bad decision, after bad decision for years, yet God remained faithful to His people. Because of His faithfulness, Joshua pleaded with them to destroy their idols and turn back to God. He unequivocally challenged them to commit their lives to the Lord.

> *So fear the Lord and serve him wholeheartedly. Put away forever the idols your ancestors worshiped when they lived beyond the Euphrates River and in Egypt. Serve the Lord alone. But if you refuse to serve the Lord, then choose today whom you will serve. Would you prefer the gods your ancestors served beyond the Euphrates? Or will it be the gods of the Amorites in whose land you now live? But as for me and my family, we will serve the Lord. (Joshua 24:14-15)*

The Israelites followed Joshua's leadership and made a covenant with God to serve Him wholeheartedly in Shechem that day. We too need to commit on a daily basis to serve the Lord and follow His leadership. Like the Israelites, it is all too easy to forget about the Lord when difficult decisions are ahead of us. The result is seldom one of peace when a decision is made without first seeking the Lord's will. *"Oh, how great are God's riches and wisdom and knowledge! How impossible it is for us to understand his decisions and his ways!" (Romans 11:33).*

In the future, our decisions need to be made in the presence of God Almighty. If we still select the wrong fork in the road, may we follow the example of the Israelites, and quickly turn back to the Lord. No matter the results, give God all honor and glory, as we continue to bloom and grow with Jesus.

Suggested Scripture Reading
- *Joshua 24:1-28*

Memorabilia

We are currently in the process of cleaning out Mom and Dad's house. Mom passed away a few years ago and Dad now lives at an assisted living facility. Some items are easy to part with while other are not. Yesterday we found a cute wooden basket and I told my sister it will hold a lot of yarn. She handed the basket back to me and said, "Yes Mary, it will hold a lot of yarn." (We both crochet.) Guess who brought the basket home? Me of course. It may or may not stay that is yet to be decided.

We have had numerous conversations like this over the past few months. You want to keep special items but at the same time you can't keep everything. The memorabilia which is dear to my heart is Mom's antique kitchen items and utensils. Many she still used and others I remember using as a kid. They now decorate a wall in my kitchen and I am thankful for the memories associated with each item. Janet and I spent many hours in the kitchen with Mom and there is probably a story to share about each item.

As we sorted more household goodies again yesterday, I posted a few items for sale on Facebook. Once again some were hard to part with but we have to draw the line somewhere. Mom had a collection of small hurricane lamps and a friend inquired about them from my post. We set a price and she was thrilled to have the collection. Tammie said she enjoys collecting the little lamps and I do not. It gave me a warm fuzzy feeling to know they were going to someone special.

The hurricane lamps are material items with sentimental value but the true value of a lamp can be found in this story found in the gospel.

> *Don't store up treasures here on earth, where moths eat them and rust destroys them, and where thieves break in and steal. Store your treasures in heaven, where moths and rust cannot destroy, and thieves do not break in and steal. Wherever your treasure is, there the desires of your heart will also be. Your eye is like a lamp that provides light for your body. When your eye is healthy, your whole body is filled with light. (Matthew 6:19-22)*

Christ is our Lamp. When we allow His light to shine through us, we glow with happiness, joy and love in a dark world of sin. When our focus remains on Christ our desire will be to shine the light for others to see.

Mom was never about material items in her life. After all she still used some of her antique kitchen utensils in the 21st century! Mom was special because of her heart and the kindness she showed others. Her eye was on the Prize, and her Lamp was Jesus Christ. Mom's biggest desire in life was to care for others and light a path of friendship along the way.

Tammie is a new Christian whose lamp shines bright for Jesus as well. She exhibits the same kindness to others as Mom did. Her love for Jesus is exuberant and evident in all she does. She is a faithful friend to many and a committed servant of Christ.

It is no coincidence that Tammie is interested in Mom's hurricane lamps. For me it was a gift from God when she purchased them. Not from a monetary standpoint but a sentimental one. These small hurricane lamps have now become a story and a devotion. A piece of my heart goes with the lamps but the example of being a shining light for Jesus will live on.

Compassion for the One

If you read my first devotional book, *Bloom Where You're Planted*, you may remember I ended at ninety-nine devotions which is an odd number and the trend continues. It comes from Jesus' parable of the Lost Sheep. Christ shared this parable to rebuke the Pharisees, but He is also speaking to you and me.

> *If a man has a hundred sheep and one of them gets lost, what will he do? Won't he leave the ninety-nine others in the wilderness and go to search for the one that is lost until he finds it? And when he has found it, he will joyfully carry it home on his shoulders. When he arrives, he will call together his friends and neighbors, saying, "Rejoice with me because I have found my lost sheep." In the same way, there is more joy in heaven over one lost sinner who repents and returns to God than over ninety-nine others who are righteous and haven't strayed away! (Luke 15:4-7)*

The book of Luke was written by Luke the physician and it is full of compassionate stories about Christ's ministry. The parable of the Lost Sheep is just one of Luke's many stories which shows Jesus' compassion for people. A compassion so deep He died a criminal's death on the cross for our sins.

Some people struggle to show compassion for others in a Christ-like manner, while others display it continually. Some believers suffer from compassion burnout. They have helped so many people do so much for so long, they have temporarily drained themselves of all empathy. No matter where you are on the compassion scale, as a servant of Christ we are called to show empathy for others, especially the lost sheep.

When we have compassion for one another it will lead to *"working together with one mind and purpose." (Philippians 2:2b)*. The main purpose of the church is to lead the lost sheep to Christ. Paul clearly gives us further instructions on how to lead those lost sheep, *"Don't be selfish...be humble...take an interest in others. You must have the same attitude that Christ Jesus had." (Philippians 2:3-4)*.

To live a Christ-like life. To pray for the lost. To offer encouragement. To love unselfishly. To comfort others. To shepherd. To humbly serve. To care about the ninety-nine sheep in the fold. To search for the lost sheep. To pray for the lost sheep. To minister to the lost sheep. It all comes down to one action—compassion. Without compassion, we have no desire to minister to others.

In order for us to remain compassionate we need to remain connected to Christ. Even Christ found time to walk away from the people and have quiet time of prayer with the Father. If you are looking for more compassion in your life start with prayer! Ask God to refresh you and give you a heart full of empathy for others. He will open your eyes to the needs of the those around you.

My reason for ninety-nine devotions is a reminder to pray for the lost sheep. So please always remember to pray for them. Our hearts need to be filled with compassion for all who need a Savior. They are the lost souls who search for a new beginning in life. A beginning which they may or may not understand starts with Christ. God is the Creator of new life. We are simply the instrument through which the lost world sees Jesus.

I pray you will stand in the gap for the lost sheep and pray for them. Ask Christ to fill you with a Christ-like compassion as you share the promise of a new life in Christ with the lost. Pray that the lost sheep will one day join the other ninety-nine in the fold because, *"There is joy in the presence of God's angels when even one sinner repents." (Luke 15:10).*

Suggested Scripture Reading
- *Philippians 2:1-11*

There are many Lost Sheep in this world who God desperately longs to comfort. That Lost Sheep may be someone you love. Why not give them the gift of the gospel message today? *Bloom Where You're Planted* and *Live Life in Full Bloom* are available at www.MaryRodman.com/shop. *"For when one lost sinner turns toward Jesus, there is wonderful rejoicing in heaven."* (Quote from devotion, "The Lost Sheep")

Conclusion—New Beginnings

Early this morning I took a drive to our shop so I could walk laps inside. It was dark outside, and the sky was so clear. It was refreshing to see the stars which shined through the morning darkness. We have had rain, snow, and a mix for several days so a clear sky was inspirational. There was a small sliver of a new moon in the sky which reminded me of new beginnings.

It is Monday morning and a new beginning to the work week. A marriage is the new beginning of a life together. A newborn baby represents the new beginning of an innocent life. It also reminded me of new beginnings which are spread throughout scripture.

Today's moon and stars were a beautiful reminder of the first creations of God. *"God made two great lights, the sun and the moon—the larger one to govern the day, and the smaller one to govern the night. He also made the stars. God set these lights in the sky to light the earth, to govern the day and night and to separate the light from the darkness. And God saw that it was good." (Genesis 1:16-18).*

Along with this new beginning came man. However, Satan deceived Adam and Eve and they brought sin into the world. The earth became so wicked God sent great flood waters to destroy all living creatures, except those which were saved on the ark with Noah and his family. God created another new beginning with Noah, a covenant to never destroy the entire earth by flood waters again. *"Yes, I am confirming my covenant with you. When I see the rainbow in the clouds, I will remember the eternal covenant between God and every living creature on earth." (Genesis 9:11a, 16).*

Good and evil continued to battle on this earth and God saw the need for a Savior. A wonderful new beginning as God became man and entered into this world as the Christ child. *"She gave birth to her firstborn son. She wrapped him snugly in strips of cloth and laid him in a manger, because there was no lodging available for them. The Savior—yes, the Messiah, the Lord—has been born today in Bethlehem, the city of David!" (Luke 2:7, 11).*

Christ taught, healed, and ministered on this earth for three years. As His ministry was coming to an end Christ offered up the cup of communion as a new covenant at the Last Supper. The bread and the wine became a symbol of His body and His blood broken and shed for the forgiveness of our sins. Communion represents a new beginning for all who believe in Christ. *"He took some bread and gave thanks to God for it. Then he broke it in pieces and gave it to the disciples, saying, 'This is my body, which is given for you. Do this in remembrance of me.' After supper he took another cup of wine and said, 'This cup is the new covenant between God and his people—an agreement confirmed with my blood, which is poured out as a sacrifice for you.'" (Luke 22:19-20).*

Christ was born of the Virgin Mary and He walked this earth as a man. When He died on the cross, He took the sins of the world upon himself. But He defeated Satan and rose again, therefore He offers each of us a new beginning. *"Because God's children are human beings—made of flesh and blood—the Son also became flesh and blood. For only as a human being could he die, and only by dying could he break the power of the devil, who had the power of death." (Hebrews 2:14).*

Jesus Christ promises a wonderful new beginning for those who put their faith and trust in Him. Your past sins are washed away and you are given a new a life with Christ! *"Since we believe that Christ died for all, we also believe that we have all died to our old life. He died for everyone so that those who receive his new life will no longer live for themselves. Instead, they will live for Christ, who died and was raised for them. This means that anyone who belongs to Christ has become a new person. The old life is gone; a new life has begun!"* (2 Corinthians 5:14b-15, 17).

As you read the stories of new beginnings spread throughout the Bible, I hope you understand God is the Creator of new beginnings. The verses I selected are just a few of many new beginnings God has offered since the beginning of time. The greatest of these new beginnings is eternal life with Christ, a new beginning which only a Savior can offer.

The new beginning of His birth. A time when God walked the earth as a man.

The new beginning of His death. He carried the sins of the world upon His shoulders when He died on the cross.

His resurrection. The new beginning in the miracle of a risen Savior. A Savior who defeated Satan and is seated at the right hand of God in heaven.

His gift of salvation. A new beginning for all. A gift which is freely given to all who ask for the forgiveness of their sins and put their hope in Jesus Christ.

I pray you understand the importance of a new life in Christ. The promise of eternity with the creator of new beginnings will change your life forever! May you seek God's presence in your life as you start each day with a new beginning and the Word of God as your guide.

Resources

After completing this devotional, I hope you rate the condition of your soul a little higher on our scale of 1-10. My goal is to motivate you and encourage you to walk closer with the Lord. Our daily lives can be difficult and frustrating but God is faithful. How you handle life's situations is directly related to the condition of your soul. In order to keep your fire burning, please connect with me at www.MaryRodman.com. There you will find more resources, such as my blog—www.MaryRodman.com/Blog, and some of my favorite quotes.

Bloom Daily Devotional Series Book 3, Bloom in God's Promises will be available in the future. Tidbits of encouragement from the book will be available on social media, or through www.MaryRodman.com/SneakPeek.

Discount Purchases

- My gift to you—Enter coupon code **ThankYou** at www.MaryRodman.com/shop to receive a ***one-time only 20% discount*** on any purchases from my website. All devotionals will be signed before shipment.
- *Bloom Daily Devotional Series Book 1, Bloom Where You're Planted*
  - "This beautifully written book is a delight, filled with wonderful stories from her life and awesome applications of God's truth. It will lift you up and speak words of truth and encouragement into your life." ~*Doris Swift*
- *Bloom Where You're Planted Journal* A quote from each devotion to journal your thoughts, includes a Daily Gratitude section.

- *Bloom Daily Devotional Series Book 2, Live Life in Full Bloom*
- *Live Life in Full Bloom Journal* Daily Gratitude and highlights from each devotion.

Download free Resources for your next event

- Free devotions from *Bloom Where You're Planted* or my free Bible study, at www.MaryRodman.com/BookBonuses
    - *Blessings* God blesses our lives every day. We need to continually watch for those blessings in the midst of our chaos.
    - *Lessons from Peter* Much like you and me, Peter had his ups and downs as a disciple of Christ, yet he led an extraordinary life. Read more devotions about the life of this great disciple in these devotions.
    - *Mary Magdalene—A Woman of Resilience* This abbreviated study walks you through the life of Mary Magdalene. She was transformed from a woman possessed by seven demons into a resilient servant of Christ.

Book Mary as a Speaker-Facilitator for your weekend retreat at www.MaryRodman.com/speaking

- ***Who Are You? Discover the woman God created you to be.*** "There are many virtuous and capable women in the world, but you surpass them all!" Proverbs 31:29
- Mary's retreat will transform your walk with Christ as she shares her funny stories, biblical examples, and powerful messages through these four topics.
    - **Defining Moments** Within minutes, the Woman caught in adultery had both good and bad defining moments in her life. The moment she was dragged into public and

humiliated, and the moment Jesus said, "Go and sin no more." Mary will challenge you to see both bad and good defining moments as good when used for God's glory.
- *God Loves You* The Samaritan Woman made many mistakes in her life, yet Jesus pursued her until she understood she was loved by the Savior of the world. Mary's words of encouragement will challenge you to serve Christ regardless of your past mistakes.
- *Who Are You?* Mary Magdalene was possessed by seven evil spirits. Christ changed her life dramatically and she understood who she was in Christ and how to serve her Savior.
- *Dare to Dream* Caleb dreamed of the Promised Land for over forty years but patiently waited for the Lord to lead the battle. Your dreams will also come into fruition when you align your dreams with God's will for your life.

- This weekend retreat is available in multiple formats.
  - Mary as a speaker. She will present the four talks and provide breakout questions for your small group leaders in advance.
  - Mary as both the speaker and the facilitator for your event.
  - Optional music by Angie Howard. Angie's musical talent as a worship leader and soloist is uplifting and inspirational.

Book Mary as a keynote speaker for your next event. Her topics include…

- *Something out of Nothing* The loss of four family members in five years sent Mary into a season of grief. Grief is a true pain which sometimes feels unbearable.

She shares how she made something out of nothing to move on with her life.

- **Dare to Dream** Your dreams are simply dreams; unless we align your dreams with God's will for your life. Mary will challenge you to accomplish great ministry when the Lord is with you. *"What you dare to dream of, dare to do." Sarah Jane Shoaf.*
- **Bloom Where You're Planted** From a wild ride down the mountains to the heartaches of life, Mary shares how to BLOOM in all aspects of your life.
- **The Woman God Sees** God sees you as His chosen, precious, beloved, royalty. Learn how *"the Lord delights in you." (Isaiah 62:4)* through Mary's personal stories intertwined with scripture.
- **A Christian Farm Wife's Perspective** As a newlywed on the farm Mary soon realized her life was much different than it was growing up on a dairy farm. She shares some of her stressful moments and how a Christ centered marriage makes a difference as they work together.
- **Faith, Farming or Career?** Do you ever wonder which direction to turn? Why not include them all? Mary's strong faith is the pivotal point which merges her farm life with her career as a writer and a speaker. She shares farm statistics to increase awareness of the family farm along with her stories of strong faith as encouragement.
- **Custom Topic** Mary enjoys Bible research and sharing some of the antics from her own life. She is open to speaking opportunities on your topic of choice. Please allow a minimum of six-weeks preparation time, unless prior arrangements have been made. For more information go to www.MaryRodman.com/speaking.

More books and resources
by Mary Rodman

Available at www.MaryRodman.com/shop

Available at www.MaryRodman.com/shop

Available at www.MaryRodman.com/shop

Coming soon…
Bloom Daily Devotional Series
Book 3 with matching journal

Inspire U

Stay in touch by using our messenger's treasury of transformational inspiration, insight, and guidance. **Download and join** the free *Inspire U app* for additional personal resources on your mobile device today!

Endnotes

[i] ORTBERG, JOHN. *SOUL KEEPING*. S.l.: BLINK, 2014.

[ii] https://www.umcdiscipleship.org/resources/history-of-hymns-nothing-but-the-blood

[iii] Lucado, Max. *He still moves stones: everyone needs a miracle*. Nashville: Thomas Nelson, 2013.

[iv] "Explore Our Bottle Cap Real Facts." Snapple. Accessed March 01, 2019. https://www.snapple.com/real-facts?gclid=CO2x9K2h4eACFYWsswod3FEN0w&gclsrc=ds.

[v] Advertisement. Http://www.azlyrics.com/lyrics/rebamcentire/hallelujahamen.html.

[vi] Advertisement. Http://www.metrolyrics.com/here-i-go-again-lyrics-whitesnake.html.

[vii] "Quotations by Author." Samahria Lyte Kaufman Quotes - The Quotations Page. Accessed July 28, 2017. http://www.quotationspage.com/quotes/Samahria_Lyte_Kaufman/.

[viii] "Scripture taken from the NEW AMERICAN STANDARD BIBLE®, Copyright ©

1960,1962,1963,1968,1971,1972,1973,1975,1977,1995 by The Lockman Foundation. Used by permission."

[ix] Brown, Robert K. *The One Year Book of Hymns*. Wheaton, Ill.: Tyndale House Publishers, 1995.

[x] Donnie Parrott - Stofcheck-Ballinger Funeral Home. Accessed June 07, 2018. http://www.stofcheck-ballinger.com/obituaries.php?action=display&id=117037.

[xi] Cooper, Herbert. *But God: Changes Everything*. Grand Rapids, MI: Zondervan, 2014.

[xii] "BibleGateway." BibleGateway.com: A searchable online Bible in over 150 versions and 50 languages. Accessed July 28, 2017. http://www.biblegateway.com/.

[xiii] http://johnmaxwellteam.com/signup-for-minute-with-maxwell.

New Living Translation
Unless otherwise indicated, all Scripture quotations are taken from the *Holy Bible*, New Living Translation, copyright © 1996, 2004, 2015 by Tyndale House Foundation. Used by permission of Tyndale House Publishers, Inc., Carol Stream, Illinois 60188. All rights reserved.

Noted as NIV
THE HOLY BIBLE, NEW INTERNATIONAL VERSION®, NIV® Copyright © 1973, 1978, 1984, 2011 by Biblica, Inc.® Used by permission. All rights reserved worldwide.

Noted as NCV

"Scripture taken from the New Century Version®. Copyright © 2005 by Thomas Nelson, Inc. Used by permission. All rights reserved."

Noted as MSG

"Scripture taken from *The Message*. Copyright © 1993, 1994, 1995, 1996, 2000, 2001, 2002. Used by permission of NavPress Publishing Group."

Noted as NKJV

Scripture taken from the New King James Version®. Copyright © 1982 by Thomas Nelson. Used by permission. All rights reserved.

www.ingramcontent.com/pod-product-compliance
Lightning Source LLC
Chambersburg PA
CBHW032103090426
42743CB00007B/221